My Feathered FRIENDS

& THE BOOK OF POEMS

PART 1

SUNIL BHATIA

PARTRIDGE

To order additional copies of this book, contact
Partridge India
000 800 10062 62
orders.india@partridgepublishing.com

www.partridgepublishing.com/india

My Feathered Friends is the story of a modern day professional who gets solace and guidance in the company of birds. Each chapter speaks of something unique which these birds have to teach us about our own abilities and leading from one event to another, unravels a world of its own. This story is dedicated to my mother who had once wished to be a bird that could flap her wings and fly away.

The Book of Poems is a collection ranging across different subjects. The writing has been kept as simple as possible so that readers of all ages can understand and find meaning in these poems.

A special word of thanks to Mrs. Amrita Chatterji and Ridhu Bhatia without whose help this book would not have come through.

Contents

My Feathered Friends Part 1

My Feathered Friends
Part 1

Chapter 1

It was a Lazy Sunday Afternoon

It was a lazy Sunday afternoon. I was half asleep after a tiring week's work. Suddenly, I heard a fluttering sound and strained to look around to the window sill. Two small pigeons had flown in and perched themselves there.

"Ah! My feathered friends! What brings you here?" said I.
They said, "We were passing by and thought of saying hello to you."

After rubbing my eyes, that were still full of sleep I said, "You have been coming before too. One morning you sat on me while I was fast asleep." Still remembered how they would fly in every morning and sit on the almirah and look at me. I would scramble to switch off the fan to save them from getting injured.

"So what's happening now? Where do you stay?"

"About half a mile away on a tree next to the community water tank"

1

Then they flew in and sat next to me on the bed.

"Actually we have a small favor from you!"
"Tell me"

"When we were very young, soon after hatching, you used to feed us along with our mom with rice and bajra. We can find the rice but are unable to find any bajra. Guess not everyone keeps it in their homes. Do you still have some left? It was damn good!"

I got up and to my joy found a small packet still left on one of the kitchen shelves. They were ecstatic and had a good feed. After some time, they said "Thank you!" and started to fly off.

"Say hi to your mom and come again!" I said.

"Sure" they said, and flew into the blue skies. I could see them getting smaller and smaller till they were merely specks and eventually vanished.

The next day, our company gave us instructions to immediately move out of the flat as our landlord was acting funny and was insistent on getting a higher rent. We moved to a new place about two miles away.

My feathered friends never came again. The only way I could identify them was by the fact that they were always together.
As of date I have kept a plate of bajra on the parapet with some water.

All kinds of birds come to feed there in the morning and wake me up with their sweet sounds. Pigeons, sparrows and even crows.
I was also able to get a sparrow shelter which now hangs next to the bajra plate.

Who knows, a sparrow just might make her nest and lay eggs there one day…

Chapter 2

Birds of a Feather

One day I got up and as usual was in a bit of a hurry to reach office. When I was having my morning cup of tea, there was the sound of a sparrow, a little louder than its usual tone.

It was complaining.

I peeked out of the window and saw that it was searching for food in the plate which I keep for them. I had forgotten to replenish it the night before.

"That crow is a thief!!!" exclaimed the sparrow glaring at the black bird which was also perched nearby. "He stole my food!"

The crow kind of huddled back at this accusation, but had no intention of leaving.

"I agree," said the society dog who used to roam around the area. "That crow ate my piece of bread that my owner's children gave me". He was kind of half asleep with his neck on the ground but his big brown eyes showed his concern as they looked up at the scene.

A majestic fat pigeon was also there, next to the sparrow, looking a trifle astonished at this early morning development, being used to the peace and quiet of old buildings where she used to stay. She was silently observing the scene all this while and taking the opportunity to peck on a few grains that were left behind.

"Calm down you two" I said as I came out to the balcony "I know this fellow," looking at the crow I said, "let's see what he has to say."

The crow was quiet for a couple of seconds and then cawed out in despair, "Nobody loves me! Everyone gives bajra to the pigeons and sparrows, and also food to the dog, but shoos us crows away. How are we supposed to live if we can't eat?"

"He has a point there." I said, "You guys should also give this poor fella a chance to have some food."

"I beg to differ" said the sparrow, "He's no 'poor fella' because he chases all the little birds away from the bajra and has a whale of a time on his own"

"Oh yeah?" said the crow, "What about the time when 10 to 12 sparrows sit on the plate at the same time and don't give others a chance?"

The situation was getting a bit out of control and I was getting late for office. "Hold it guys, let's come to some understanding as I have to rush. I'll put some more bajra for the sparrow and pigeons and a chapatti for the crow, after this no fighting!"

The dog also got up in anticipation with his tongue hanging out as he started panting in excitement. "You'll also get something my friend." I said with a grin.

I could see the community having their breakfast as I zipped out of my apartment to go to work.

"So much for a start to this day" I thought. "I wonder what's lined up in the days to come. The forecasts say that the monsoon is arriving in the next four days. I shouldn't forget to get some more bajra on my way back home. God, I have an evening meeting and may get delayed, I hope the shops are open at that time! We'll see…"

It so happened that I could bring the bajra that night and got a good response the next morning. Eight to ten sparrows and a few pigeons, but no crow. As they say the crow is considered the most intelligent of all birds. He started sitting on the kitchen window sill and cawing there.

A one legged sparrow would also come once in a while. I guess she was like that since birth. Nevertheless this congregation or as they say 'birds of a feather' made things more interesting!

One morning a bunch of pigeons were cooing as they pecked at the plate.

"This god damn city life is killing me" said one of them. "You have to really be the early bird to catch the worm."

"There's too much competition."

"I wish I was back in the park where I grew up."

A fourth pigeon flew in and held on to a tree branch nearby.

They stopped and one pigeon exclaimed "Its Mr. Lova Lova!"

This fourth pigeon which was, apparently, male was trying his luck in finding a partner. He would take a little flight up, glide around and then land again after which he would start cooing. I think he was trying to impress the ladies. He also brought a twig after his second flight, perhaps to show his nest building skills.

All this would surely add to the fun of watching my feathered friends, but the fast pace of life was getting to be a too much for me. I needed to get away for a day or two, so decided to go out for a weekend vacation with a few friends and relatives.

As I was packing my bags I thought of taking a look to see if everything was ok at the balcony. Well, it was all normal. The sparrow shelter was still empty and the birds had made quite a mess with their droppings.

Suddenly the society dog started barking. I looked down and saw a little pigeon on the floor. She seemed to be unwell as she was unable to fly. I rushed down and after picking her up landed in a little animal hospital. They gave her some medicine, tagged her leg and gave me a number after recording the case.

"You can check her condition after a few days" said the Doctor. I took their numbers for future reference.

After getting back, I left for a 2 day camping trip to the outskirts of Mumbai and upon my return forgot about this incident, work taking a priority.

It was the usual rushed up day and I was to meet an important client, when a pigeon chose to shower its droppings on me. A colleague had once told me that it meant good luck... And this was an important deal that meant a lot to our organization.

We got the deal!

I was so overjoyed that I bought a double helping of bajra that evening and the moment I reached home, there was a huge downpour. The monsoons had begun.

The rain gods decided to go on a short vacation after a few days and I was finally able to hear some 'chirrups' now and then. It was still not easy to spot any of my feathered friends as they had tucked themselves comfortably in cozy nooks and corners all around the nearby buildings. I would still keep some bajra, hoping that the bird shelter would get a visitor sooner or later.

The season change led me to being at home for a few days as the 'viral fever' that was doing the rounds. On the fourth day of my recovery I suddenly remembered the pigeon that I had left at the animal clinic a week ago, so I went on to pay her a visit. As things turned out to be, she had made a complete recovery. The vet promptly handed her over to me and told me to "take care!" As we drove back home, the creature was quietly seated on top of the chair next to me looking out of the car window.

"Why are you so quiet?" I said, "You're OK now right?"

She glanced at me and said with a sigh "Yes, I'm fine, but I'm just wondering about you people,"

"What do you mean?"

"I wonder how you humans live with all this traffic. I mean it really must be difficult getting around. You are really not free !!!"

"Now we have a philosophical one here," I thought "but she was right"

"Well you're not entirely wrong," I had reached home by then and put her on the living room sofa, "But we manage to find our way through."

I opened the windows for some fresh air. The pigeon flew and sat on top of the TV as it started raining again.

"Why don't you find a partner?" I asked, "I'm sure there are more pigeons in the sky than there are humans on the earth." I wouldn't know if it was true but I just said it to liven up the conversation.

"I had one," she said "But he flew away."
"I'm sorry to hear that, but..if you don't mind my asking, what happened?" I sat down with glass of juice after feeding the fish in the living room. They had hungrily come up the tank as soon as they saw me enter.

"We met on a roof top two months ago where we had an instant liking for each other. He would entertain me with his lively sounds and we would both fly around searching for food. We even sneaked out one evening to the nearby watering hole for some peace and quiet away from the city hubbub."

"And then?" I asked.

The pigeon was looking out into the emptiness of the dark rainy skies. "We started having a few differences."

"Ah! Like we humans also have. What kind of differences?"

"He wanted to go forty miles south to a more bustling area downtown, whereas I wanted to stay in and around this area. He would always say he's got to go where there's a future, and this part of the city was run down." She started sniffing as her eyes became watery.

"Here take some water it'll make you feel better. You still want to talk about it?"

She pecked at the water in the little bowl that I had placed in front of her for a while, and then said, "Yes. After a long time I had found someone whom I thought I could be with and he seemed to be the perfect person for me..."

"So where was the problem?" I began feeling a little guilty for getting inquisitive but couldn't control myself, "He liked you too, right?"

She looked at me straight in the eye with a tear drop rolling down her little beak, came closer and almost whispered in my ear, "There was another pigeon that was after him too!"

My jaw dropped down in astonishment. "How can you be so sure?"

"He started acting strangely after the first 5-6 weeks of our being together and would make an excuse to leave every time we met. Infact I saw them together by the School building in the next block."

"That's OK they may have just been old friends." I said. "Was there anything else?" My guilt seemed to increase even more but at the same time I felt like a counselor for this creature in distress.

"He said he'd seen a window sill on the 37th floor of a flat next to the sea where he wanted to nest but I like interiors where its warmer. We just had the opposite ideas for everything we wanted. We started disagreeing on small things like choice of food, places to go, even on the location of our nest."

"That's normal. We are all different in our own way. That is why we all have our disagreements."

"But that other pigeon made things worse! I even started spying on them morning and night!"
"And what did you conclude by this?"

"They were quite...friendly."

"When is the last time you both met?"

"The day you took me to the hospital, he just said he needed to get some fresh air and I have not seen him since then. It made me really sick. By the way, thanks for helping me out that day."

"Don't mention it. Where do you think he is now?"

"I can't say, maybe with his 'friend', I really don't know what to do."

There was a little silence in the room, then a small voice came from the fish tank.

"Dump the bugger. That's what he deserves!"

We turned to see that one of the goldfish had spoken. The 7 other fish had also gathered together in the aquarium as they had been listening to our conversation.

In fact, I noticed that they hadn't even touched the food that I had put for them. They were probably having a discussion about the pigeon amongst themselves.

"How can you say that? Maybe he really loves her."

"Now that is a dumb statement. Can't you see he's already with that other pigeon?"

"I agree, these males I tell you! They are all the same! One of them swam me around a pond for a full week until he started fancying another goldfish! Just can't wait to get my fins on him!"

The Red Cap Fish seemed a little unconvinced with all this talk and looked a little thoughtful.

"What do you have to say?" I asked.

"I think, she's jumping to conclusions. Maybe the other pigeon is just a friend. I'll tell you what, you should give each other some space, take time to understand each other and respect your differences. Have you asked him about this other pigeon?"

"Yes I did, twice, he just shrugged it off, and changed the conversation" said the pigeon.

"Why don't you just do what he wants, like what he likes? Maybe then he would start appreciating your gestures and open up more with you!"

"But I can't just give in every time." The pigeon had come closer to the aquarium to speak with the Red Cap. The other fish seemed to have forgotten the whole incident and started going after the fish food.

"Listen girlie, if you want something in life you have to go after it and do whatever it takes to get it. You may have to make a lot of sacrifices on the way. Life isn't easy and you have to also be ready to face the consequences of your decisions and actions. One of them would be to just sit and pity yourself, the other would be to go out and get the person you like."

I excused myself, as I had to take my medicine from the other room and check my mails. I came back after half an hour to the living room but couldn't see the pigeon anywhere.

"Hey, where's the pigeon gone?" I asked the fish.

The Red Cap gave me a beaming smile as she gracefully moved her tail and side fins in the water "She's gone to find her partner."

"All's well so far!" I said to myself as it was time to retire for the day. As I was closing the balcony doors of the living room, I heard the faint sound of a conversation from the fish tank.

"That was a fine bit of advice you gave to the pigeon," one of the goldfish was saying to the Red Cap, "But let me tell you something, it wasn't the right advice."

The Red Cap calmly looked at the Goldfish and said "What do you mean?"

"Look, she's gone out to search for a partner who doesn't give a damn for her, on top of that he's seeing someone else. Don't you think it's just a wild goose chase? I mean the poor girl's going to run after someone who may not even be interested in her."

I quietly sat down on the sofa trying to figure out this new turn of events. The Goldfish was not exactly wrong either.

The Red Cap promptly replied "That's just what you think. If he didn't like her why did they tag along all this while? The very fact that he was meeting her till last week was only because he was or rather is still interested in her."

"That's very sweet, but if he really liked her, then why was he seeing this 'other' friend? I'd rather say that our Dear Mr. Pigeon is a double timing twit and our little friend is ruining her life by going after him."

The Red Cap was still calm. "I had thought about that too, but it would be wrong to label someone based on only what you've heard."

"Heard? I thought she said she saw them! In fact she actually saw them many times. Didn't you hear that? She had actually spied on them!"

The Red Cap heaved a sigh and said, "What she saw may not have been what she thought she saw."

"Quite a nice riddle! If you may, would you please elaborate on that in simpler words?"

For me, this conversation was much more entertaining than watching TV.

"Quite simply, she has not attempted to understand her mate and he is getting suffocated because of this. He therefore, goes to the other pigeon, who is more understanding and may have known him since earlier days. It's just a basic relationship problem which can be worked out."

My weary eyes opened as this dawned upon me..it was way past midnight, but this was far too interesting for me to go to sleep.

The Goldfish was still adamant," But if what you are saying is not true, then the girlie is in for a tough time chasing something she'll never get. She's simply wasting her time and emotions."

The Red Cap took another deep breath, "What you say is also a possibility, but we should always follow what we like, in this case she likes him and he has not actually told her that he is leaving her. She just has to try again and keep on doing it. Perhaps his other friend is really only a friend. He still may be liking our pigeon friend but for certain aspects of her which she can work upon. If she doesn't even try that's worse."

The Goldfish was not convinced at all, "She won't get him!".

The Red Cap started to slowly swim around. "I hope she does, rather, I think she will!"

I got up and went to bed. As I switched off the lights, I thought to myself, "I also don't know if she'll get him, but I hope she does."

Chapter 3

The Parrot

I was woken up one Sunday morning by some shrill sounds. I had never heard anything like that before and tossing in bed tried catching up on some more sleep.

As I wearily tried looking out of the window our maid said, "Parrots!" She was fixing breakfast for us flat mates in the kitchen. I looked at her through half closed eyes, "Parrots? What are they doing here? I thought they were supposed to be in...... people's houses."

"Not all of them," said the Bai, still busy making parathas for us.

Since I had never quite seen a parrot up close in many years, I dragged myself out from under the blankets and strained to see in the direction of the sound.

A flurry of bright green color hit my eyes and I picked up my glasses for a better view.

It was quite an amazing sight to see 8 or 10 bright green parrots perched on a tree creating perfect cacophony on a quiet Sunday morning. Somehow the dreary people around never seemed to mind.

Suddenly, they flew from the tree in direction of my window and as they did, one of them actually came quite close to me.

"Hello!" I said in a fairly loud voice.

He stopped and sat on a branch near my window.

I again said "Hello!" (It sounded rather like "helllewww!!!")
Within 5 seconds the parrot replied "helllewww!!!"

"How dooo you dooo?" It again answered, "How dooo you dooo?"

I chuckled, remembering how we in our school days used to repeat what our teachers were teaching a similar way. In fact some students were known to be like parrots as they could memorize entire books and write the same in the exams. We could also remember entire mathematical procedures, even if we didn't understand a thing and would eventually forget it all once the exams were over.

"Can you think?" I asked the parrot. He just repeated as usual in his squawky voice, "Can you think?"

Our maid came to the window and gave a few chilies to the bird. He pecked on them for some time seemingly enjoying every bite that he took as he held on to them with his talons. He suddenly realized that he was left behind by his friends, so he flew away, with a chilly in his beak.

"Breakfast's ready" said the maid and left.

As I sat down to have some, I began thinking....school? It was in college. No, wait, maybe it was at my first job... God, it's still the same! We have to go through painfully thick manuals, mugging up procedures, take exams to qualify and feel dejected if we don't do well.

Are we all any better than these parrots? I guess it's a trap for us lesser mortals, created by those higher up.

I was still feeling tired as the parrot alarm woke me up earlier than I would on a Sunday.

And, before long, I was again in the world of dreams...

Chapter 4

The Strange Dream

It was a strange dream... I was walking through a dense forest and the deeper I went the brighter it became.

The usual sounds of birds and scurrying animals were adding to the intense experience. I arrived to a beautiful waterfall where birds were diving in and out of the the and pool below and many more sat on the rocks around.

My gaze suddenly went to a large falcon sitting on top of the highest rock looking around with an air of profundity. He turned and looked straight at me.

"What brings you here my friend?" He asked.

I was a bit awestruck by his presence but said, "Well this is a dream, and somehow, I've ended up at this place."

"Yes, people come to this place only in their dreams and they never go back."

"What do you mean?"

"You will never be able to come out of this dream."

"Are you serious? I have a presentation due tomorrow and I also have to visit the dentist."

The falcon seemed unperturbed by my words and after a few seconds said "Everyone who comes here says such things."

"But this is a dream right?"

"No. Your life is the dream…This is for real…"

I was beginning to get more and more intrigued by what it was saying, so I stepped over the rocks and came closer to the falcon.

My mind was brimming with thoughts like, "What is this place? Where am I now? How did I reach here?, I know not how.."

The falcon replied, "We all belong here. You are in the place where we all stay together, in happiness."

The falcon had heard my thoughts. The forest was very beautiful, serene and mysterious at the same time.

"Why are there no humans here?"

"No humans only birds."

"Then why am I here?"

"You're a bird as well."

"What!?" I looked down to see my hands and feet, instead I saw some feathers and claws."

This was all really unbelievable. "But this is a dream right?" I was beginning to get a little concerned.

The falcon again replied "No. Your life is the dream… This is for real…"

I fluttered my wings, rose above the forest and got a view of the ocean, mountains and clear blue skies. It was wonderful to be free from everything and just to be flying around.

Suddenly there was a shrill sound which rang through the skies. Everything vanished.

I was back in my room and the doorbell was ringing.

Chapter 5

The Tale of Missy Pigeon

Some friends had arrived so I got ready to move out for the evening. We went to a nearby restaurant to have some nice seafood and beer as it was our favorite haunt. While we chatted through the evening, my mind kept drifting to the strange dream. It was a little hard to believe that this was reality. The dream was still fresh in my mind and I wondered what the falcon meant when he said "Your life is the dream… This is for real."

We wound up early as the 'Monday blues' feeling was beginning to creep up and found myself at home again looking out into the endless night, when I heard a fluttering sound.

It was the pigeon who had gone searching for her partner..
"What a pleasant surprise! Welcome back my friend…welcome back." She responded to my greeting with a little nod.

"Were you able to find your partner?"

"You were right" she said, "The other pigeon is just a friend."

"That's good, so how're things with Mr. Pigeon then?"

She took a deep breath and said "She's too possessive about him, I mean their friendship..."

I began understanding her plight and could actually empathize with her,
"And does that bother you?'

"Well it does... I spoke to him on these concerns and he assured me that she's nothing more than a friend."

It seemed like a deadlock situation.

"I told you the poor thing was wasting her time going after Mr. Pigeon" The goldfish said to the Red Cap fish.

We were all in the living room pondering over the situation. The Red Cap had swum away from the other fish to a corner of the aquarium apparently mulling over the pigeon's plight.
"What else did he tell you?" The Red Cap asked the Pigeon.

"He doesn't talk much with me, things are not quite like they used to be."

"I'm sure they're not, however, he does still meet you right?"

"Yes."

"So where's the problem?"

"He doesn't give me enough time, rather he spends more time with his *friend*."

"If you, for an instance, believe that he still likes you, would it make things better?"

The pigeon thought for a little while, "Perhaps," she finally said.

"Then why don't you think happy thoughts?"

"But reality is different." The pigeon seemed to be seeing things in a mature manner.

"Reality is what you make it to be. Keep the belief that your pigeon still likes you. For if he didn't he wouldn't come back to you.." That sounded convincing enough.

The Red Cap seemed to be giving some sound advice to Missy Pigeon.

"But why does he still go to her?"

"Because she's his friend"

"And what about me?"

"You're the bird he likes."

I excused myself as I had to crash for the night. Thoughts were getting jumbled up in my sleepy brain "Your life is the dream... This is for real... Reality is what you make it to be..."

Before long, sunlight floated in through the curtains and Monday had arrived. Another week at work. Life became terribly busy. I began wondering how I was even getting time to breathe.

It had almost become a routine affair. I would come home late at night, switch on the aquarium light and see the fish swimming around normally after they got attuned to the brightness. I would sometimes sit there for almost an hour and watch them move around effortlessly. The serenity along with the voice of the bubbling water through the aerator would help soothe my nerves.

I had come to know from them that Missy Pigeon had been visiting them during the day time to get further 'guidance' on her personal life.

On one such evening when I entered the house, I could hear the voice of the Pigeon and Redcap fish in the dark. They looked at me when I turned the lights on and I just signaled them to carry on as I went in for a shower.

After returning to the living room, I tried getting a hang of where the story of the pigeon was headed.

"I don't know why this is happening to me!" The pigeon was looking a bit distressed. "I just liked him and have to go through all this."

"Now now.." The Red Cap fish was consoling her, "I just think you're overreacting to this whole incident."

"That other pigeon is not leaving him alone, why can't she just realize that he now belongs to me?"
"Aha! That's where you're making a mistake, he doesn't belong to you, you don't possess him. It seems like you're the one who is over possessive, not the other pigeon."

Missy Pigeon was just engrossed in her own conversation

"Even the one legged sparrow found a partner. He came from a nearby village and guess what? He also had one leg! They both seemed so happy together, all the other birds were congratulating them yesterday outside, on the parapet."

"Yes we all saw it," said the Red Cap, "But you should not compare."

"I guess I am not that good looking" said the pigeon morosely, "She has a better plumage than mine, maybe he likes her feathers more than mine."

"There's no need for getting paranoid. He liked you that's why he met with you the first time. Perhaps you are changing by getting worked over this whole thing, and he doesn't see the same pigeon he liked."

"The Red Cap is right," I was thinking to myself.

"What should I do now?" It seemed that the Pigeon had just surrendered at this point of time.

"Just go out, get some fresh air and exercise and become the pigeon that you were before. Look what you've done to yourself! He is seeing now that you are not the pigeon he liked once, carefree and happy."

"It's not easy to be happy."

"It is. Just forget everything and fly out, the way you used to before you met him. He just might see you the way he did the first time he saw you."

"The Red Cap seems to be right" I couldn't help interrupting at this point of time.

"Ok." said the pigeon without further ado and flew out.

"The poor thing is still wasting her time" The goldfish swam closer to the Red Cap. "When will you guys learn? I just don't believe it!" She turned to look in my direction. "I know you also believe in the Red Cap's talks... You guys are all nuts!"

She waved her fins in exasperation and moved away to another side of the aquarium.

I started smiling to myself.

Missy Pigeon was there one afternoon having bajra on the parapet.

It was a public holiday, so once I sat on the balcony with the newspaper, the sight of her caught my eye. She was with the other birds and seemed to look OK, unlike the last time I had seen her.

"Hello there, nice to see you back. How's life?" I said cheerfully. She looked at me and said "I'm fine thanks" and continued on with her meal.

Curious as I was, I ended up asking, "So how's your friend doing?"

"Oh he's fine!" To my surprise, she was not reacting in her usual way and continued relishing the bajra. This increased my curiosity further, so I went out near her and asked "So what happened with you two then?"

"Nothing."

"Nothing? How can nothing happen? I mean something would have happened!"

"No not really... well, I gave him an ultimatum."

"You what?"

"I told him it was me or her."
"That's gutsy, so what happened after that?"

"Nothing. Things were still the same."

"And it doesn't bother you?"

"Not really, I have just stopped worrying about this."

"But that's not easy. I thought you were quite 'caught up' in this whole thing. How did you do it?"

For the first time she stopped eating and looked up at me "I just changed the way I thought."

"Hmm... If I may ask in what way?"

"I realized that I was ruining my peace of mind by unnecessarily involving myself."

She seemed to have grown in years.

"But, how can you be so cool, even if what the Goldfish said was true? You know what I mean.."

I looked back at the aquarium. The fish were taking a nap as they had come to the bottom of the tank and seemed motionless.

The pigeon finished her lunch and flew to the railing where I was standing.

"I have realized that I had been wasting my time over this whole affair. What the Goldfish was saying was right, but not totally."

"How's that?"

"My friend does meet his friend but I realized that he needs that space."

"And?"

"I have realized that it's better to just let him go. He loves his freedom you know! I have also realized one more thing, that it's not worth wasting today. I have started living one day at a time. If he's meant to come back to me, he will.. If he won't, I'll just consider him as a friend whom I met." I felt a little relieved, seeing her better now as she flew away.

I had my lunch and decided to take a nap. "*It's not worth wasting today*" the words of the pigeon kept ringing in my ears.

I started thinking "I have to put my clothes in the washer, visit the mall, buy some fruit on the way back. It's not worth wasting today for tomorrow is another busy day."

Chapter 6

The Friendly Owl conversations and a Twist in the Tale

Since the days were getting a bit over packed, with too much work and too little time, I discovered a new way to get a little relaxation. I would take a stroll late in the night with the cool breeze rustling through the leaves along the way.

As I sat on one of the benches, a pleasant hooting sound greeted me through the darkness. After straining my eyes through the black night, a pair of large round eyes met mine.

An owl was sitting on one of the branches of the tree in front of me.
"How are you friend?" I greeted him.

"I am fine."

"Do you usually come out this time of the night?"

"Yes I do."

"Don't you feel lonely sitting there all alone?"

"I could ask you the same question," he replied promptly.

"My story's different, I've had one of *'those days'* at work, you know what I mean?"

"Well, I come out at this time because this is when I can do what I want to do and be who I want to be. It's also a lot more peaceful at this time." The owl gave me a knowing grin.

"I suppose what you say is true, we all need some time to forget what we've become, remember who we were and be who we are." I was totally lost in the blissful night.

The owl gave a few more hoots before turning to me again.

"You seem to look a bit tired."

"Yes, life can take its toll on you at times. It's the same thing every day, work, clients, targets, phone calls, meetings. It never seems to end."

The Owl gave one more hoot after which it said "You take life too seriously."

I was caught by surprise ."And how can you say that?"

"I've seen you a couple of times coming home late. You are giving more time to your work than is required."

"Life is competitive you know, one has to work hard to make a living."

The Owl nodded his head in agreement. "That is right but it should not be at the cost of your personal space and desires."

"But how do I do the things that I want? One needs enough time to do that. By the end of the day I'm too tired to do anything."

"You have to find and make time for yourself."

"Thanks for the advice friend. Adieu for the time being. I have to crash now as I have an early morning appointment with a client."

"You're most welcome," said the owl and continued with his sweet hooting.
As I returned home and opened the front door, I saw the fish together in the tank. A serious discussion was on.

"Where were you?" The Red Cap fish asked me.

"Why? What happened?"

The fish looked at each other and then the Gold fish said to the Red Cap fish "You tell him."

By this time I had my arms out asking them "what's happening?'

The Red Cap finally said, "Mr. Pigeon had come a short while ago."
"Mr. Pigeon? Oh you mean Missy Pigeon's 'Mr.' Pigeon. He must've found out that she has been visiting us.

"Yes he did."

"And why did he come here?"

"He says that he's been searching for her for the last two weeks and can't find her anywhere!"

The Owl conversations.

One night, stepping out to for a walk, I remembered the Owl and decided to look for him.
I found him on the same tree, hooting occasionally in the stillness of the night. He appeared like a hermit absorbed in his solitude,

perhaps thinking of ways and means to unravel the questions and mysteries of life.

That night even the crickets were unusually quiet, maybe due to the weather change over the last few days.

"Hello!" I greeted the Owl

"Hello!" He replied and looked at me with an intense gaze, then said "You've come to ask me some questions." I noticed how he didn't ask me this but in fact stated it, like he knew what was on my mind.

"Yes" I replied.

"Sure! So what's it about, work, life or love?"

I tried to gather my thoughts and emotions.. "It's about life."

"You want to know why you're sitting at this time of the night, talking to an owl when you could have well been happily tucked away, sleeping in bed, right?"

"Yes."

"What do you think is the answer to this question?'
"I don't know, perhaps I'm a bit confused about a few things in life."

"Like?"

"Like being happy and getting satisfaction out of life. Is it really hard to find happiness?"

"Depends on what you want in life." The Owl seemed to have a very clear mind.

"I know what I want, perhaps know how to get it. Is it really important to get what you want?"

"Depends on how much you want it"

"Can I live without getting my wants?"

"If you know how to be happy without them"

"That is impossible!"

"No it's not"

"How can you say that?" By now I had come to the end of the seat trying to hear the Owl properly.

"You are sitting at this time of the night, listening to an Owl. Where are your wants now?"

"I don't know"

"That's it! Are you happy at this point of time?"

"Yes, maybe…"

"That answers your question."

The Owl flapped his wings and looked at me again. As I got up to leave still in some thought, the Owl said "The Red Cap fish was right, but the Goldfish too was not wrong."

I turned around in astonishment...

As I looked at the Owl in amazement, he seemed unaware of my reaction as he gave out one more hoot, filling the night with a beautiful sound which travelled through its magical darkness.

He looked at me and gave a little smile.

"How did you know that?" I demanded to know.

"When the world is awake and talking in the day, I'm quiet and hear a lot of things."

"And how did you hear so much that you know so much?"

"We owls have Binocular Vision. I can see a hundred times better than you in the dark. I also have binocular hearing".

"Hearing?"

"Yes, we can hear ten different sounds at the same time. I don't always sit on this branch, I have also been near your home at times."

"But still, how do you know so much?"

"I have friends too you know. We owls have strong communication skills."

I broke out into a laugh. It was so simple. "What else do you know?" All this seemed very amusing to me suddenly.

"Why do you want to know?" The Owl had a knowing look on his face

"Human beings are quite inquisitive you know."

"Is it necessary that you know?"

"Well actually...no"

"Then let's change the topic, for sometimes it's better to know as much as is required.."

I gave a long look at the Owl and after a gentle nod said "I must say, you're an interesting bird."

"Why do you say so?"

"Because you know so much. I wish we all knew more."

The Owl, who also seemed to be enjoying our conversation said, "You can."

"How?"

"By talking less and listening more."

I pondered over what it said and agreed "Yes that makes sense."

It was way past midnight and realized that had to get asleep.

I thanked the Owl and started to leave..when a thought came to my mind.

I turned back and after reaching the branch asked the Owl "Can I ask you a question?"

The Owl was quiet and did not reply immediately. After a while, he said

"You want to know where Missy Pigeon is..."

The Owl's Confession.

"Yes" I said without much hesitation.

"We Owls have a principle that even if we have and share information internally, we will never interfere in the personal affairs or lives of other creatures."

"But you are not interfering. I am only asking you to tell me if you know where Missy Pigeon is."

"I can't, I am bound by the oath of the Owl congregation."

"Which means that you know where she is."

"Yes."

"Aww... come off it, what's there to be so secretive about? At least tell me if she's ok?"

"Yes, she's fine."

"Then why did Mr. Pigeon come back searching for her?"

"You are asking too many questions.."

"I have to, as you would agree and appreciate, I have spent some amount of time with Missy Pigeon and you could say that I'm asking out of concern. Even the fish at home are wanting to know."

The Owl was silent for some time. Then he said, "Ok, there's a possibility for us Owls to speak out. But only in exceptional cases."

A sigh of relief came to me.

"I must confess that Missy Pigeon was also visiting me and some elderly Owls as she was going through a tough time. Sometime ago, she met another Pigeon who became her friend and helped her out of her condition."
"So she's gone with him?"
"Well that is not easy to say but she found some solace in his company."

"And why did Mr. Pigeon come back that night searching for her? Wasn't he happy with his other 'friend'?"

"Well she was his childhood friend. She flew away with a Royal Pigeon."

"Royal Pigeon?" That was something I had never heard before.

"Yes, he was from the lineage of the Royal family of Pigeons from an Old Maharaja's pet collection living in a neighboring state. It seems he stays at the Maharaja's Bungalow and has a good lifestyle there."

"Oh, I see." I shook my head, "It also happens with us humans in real life here."

The Owl continued with his story, totally engrossed in it. "So Mr. Pigeon realized that Missy Pigeon was his true partner and has been searching for her since then as he's been left all alone now."

I looked at the Owl, "And now he can't find her."

"Exactly."

"Will Missy Pigeon come back?"

The Owl again gave the knowing smile to me and said

"For that you'll have to wait and see..."

Chapter 7

The Swan on the Lake

I had to go out of town to visit our business partners. On my way back I took an old route in the evening where there was a large pond where birds used to come for a drink of water. I spotted a swan and went and sat next to her.

"You're new here," the swan said, "I haven't seen you here before."

"Yes my dear, just thought of coming by this area as it's quiet and peaceful."

"It sure is, we also come here every year. But I must tell you that a lot has changed though."

"In what way?"

"The air used to be a lot cleaner earlier. Even this pond...things are not the same"

"You are right, we humans are to blame for that. We are all out to ruin this lovely planet."

The swan looked at me with some concern and said "You know we are nearly extinct in some parts of the world."

"Yes I'm aware. But there are some good people also who are trying to conserve nature"

The swan showed me the other swans. "Look at us, if we didn't fly here, what would become of us?"
"Yes, I suppose you have to, because of climate"

"Yes that is a reason why we swans fly here in the winters"

"Oh yes! I have read somewhere that you are migratory birds. Some of you fly many miles from the northern hemisphere to warmer countries. How do you make it so far?"

"We have to do it in order to survive, we need to get to warmer places for food, water and shelter. Flying is no problem you see.. after all we are birds. We just stick around together and make it."

"Wow! And you're swimming so peacefully in this pond as if you had to make no effort to come this far."
"It only takes effort when you unwillingly do something."

The bird's words made me curious and I wanted to know more, "Could you elaborate on that please?"

"When you are doing something for the sake of doing it, you are making an effort."

The swan swam away and after making a circle came back again.

This set me thinking for some time. When the swan came back, I asked her, "But without any effort we can't get anything. Right?"

The swan answered back, "What are you trying to get?"

I cleared my throat and said "I'm trying to get what every average ambitious and educated human being wants, a decent lifestyle, money, a little recognition, maybe a better car, also some good vacations, the love of friends and family and..."

I turned to the swan and saw that she was smiling..."And?" She said.

"Well the list can actually go on." I could feel a lump form in my throat. "But why do you ask?"

"I ask because I wanted to know if you have to make an effort to get all this." The swan was somehow still smiling.

I put on a brave face, "Of course one has to make an effort to get all this. One has to toil so much in today's world to get the basic necessities of life."

"May I ask you another question?"

"Sure"

"What are the things that you can do without making an effort?" This caught me completely off guard and got the gears in my head moving.

"Well..you can say things like humming a tune, watering the plants, playing with a roadside cat, patting a dog, talking to people, maybe writing down something. There are many more things that I do without making any effort."

The swan after listening intently asked "Just one last question, why do you think you don't need to make any effort in doing these things?"

I replied almost immediately "Because..because I like doing these things!!!"

No sooner had I said this, than the truth dawned upon me and the realization kept me still for several moments.
"But, these things can't give me all those things that I just told you about. Right?" I looked at the swan challengingly.

"Yes they can't, but perhaps one of them can."

I was not fully convinced and said "These are all what we may call hobbies or our natural inclinations."

"Yes, natural inclinations, you are right." I could see where the swan was headed. We all have natural inclinations, which we tend to forget, or ignore."

I pointed out to the swan "Yes, but why are these inclinations so important? We love doing what comes naturally, but what's that got to do with what we want to get in life?"

The swan came closer to me and said almost in a whisper

"In simpler words you may say, this is your free spirit!"

"Free spirit?"

That sounded like magic to my ears. Now that's what we all need, a free spirit.

"Now I have to ask you a question." This time I was smiling at the swan "If according to you being in our 'Free Spirit' is so easy, then why is it so difficult in real life, why are we still unable to get into this so called 'Free Spirit?'

"Good question," said the swan.

"So?" I was looking at the swan as if I'd just check mated her at a game of chess.

"The answer is that it's not difficult, in fact quite easy to get into your free spirit."

My head started to spin a bit "Oh really? And how is that, if I may ask so?"

It' easy. The only thing is that we just start getting involved in things that cause us misery."

Now my head was definitely spinning but I wasn't going to give up so easily on this discussion "Look friend, misery, pain, whatever you may call is all a part of life."

The swan coolly said "Not necessarily."

My mouth hung open in disbelief, "Now that's something that I find hard to believe"

"Ok, let me explain," The swan almost appeared like a tutor in a class explaining the answer to a pupil, "How was your day today?"

"Well, it was so so, some great moments, some not so great. In fact, now that I think about it, they weren't all that good at all."

The swan asked again "When these not so good incidents happened, were they really not so good or were you able to cope with them?"

"We'll if I had a better frame of mind, perhaps could have coped with them better. I could have handled the situations in a better manner."

"And when are you in the best frame of mind?" Now I was thoroughly confused and everything seemed to be swimming in front of me.

"When I'm calm, composed, non-judgmental with myself and also perhaps when I'm a bit excited and enthusiastic as well"

I stopped after that.

The swan said "Let me ask you just one more question."

"Ok…" My mind was a bit numb by now, as I spoke in a feeble voice.

"Have you ever noticed that some people appear to be calm, composed, non-judgmental, with themselves and perhaps a bit excited and enthusiastic more than other people that you see around you? And this has got nothing to do with all what they have or don't have, and irrespective of the situation that they are in or out of."

"Yes."

"These are the people who live with their free spirit!"

Chapter 8

Dinner with the Copper fish

I found myself at home the next evening having dinner along with the fish in the living room. I had picked up a pizza enroute from the nearest Dominoes store.

As I put some fish food in the tank, and narrated the story of the Swan to the fish, I got a fins up (their version of thumbs up.)

The Copper fish even went to the extent of saying that the swan could say such things because she was in her elements.

I couldn't have agreed more with this. The other fish were almost dozing off but the Copper fish was still awake.

"I must tell you that you humans have got it all wrong!" the Copper fish was swimming close to the tank wall as he said all this to me

"What do you mean?" The other fish were sound asleep by now.

"You humans tend to lose it, I mean you lose your spirit somewhere along the way."

I kept quietly munching on the Pizza as the Copper fish continued.

"You all seem to be fine till the time you are children, but once you grow up… I tell you!!!"

I had no choice but to continue quietly eating the pizza.

I finally broke my silence, "But we all have to grow up don't we?"

"Yes," said the Copper fish. "Grow up, not grow out of yourselves."

"But life is change and change is life isn't it? I mean how can you expect me to behave like a 5 year old kid?"

"That's the whole problem," the Copper fish swam to catch some fish food. It came back after gobbling down three little grains and said, "That's the whole problem. You humans think that growing up is losing the child in you, but it's not. It's keeping the child in you alive. But you can't do it as everyone around you isn't doing it either."

I picked up one more slice of pizza after sprinkling some chili flakes and oregano seasoning on it.

"And you all turn into monsters once you grow up!"

All this sounded like food for thought.

I gave the Copper fish two more fish food pellets as a mark of appreciation for all that he had told me. "You guys have got it all wrong…" The Copper fish thus ended the conversation as I wished him and the others a very good night and switched off the aquarium lights with a "Thank you friend!"

"No mention" Said the Copper fish in the Dark. "Sweet Dreams."

I was almost beginning to feel like a child after this experience. As I lay in bed waiting to go to sleep, I felt a sense of happiness and gratitude. Happiness for having these wonderful friends around and gratitude for their candour and honesty in saying what they believed was true.

Chapter 9

Mrs. Sparrow

I had a three day long weekend holiday. On one of those days I particularly noticed a sparrow that had a louder voice than the others. At first I thought that she was the youngest of the lot and was trying to seek the attention of the others. Later, I found out that she was actually the eldest, with five siblings.

For the purpose of this story, we shall call her 'Mrs. Sparrow'

"Now now, everyone take turns to feed, children go slow, don't gobble the bajra too fast." She seemed to be seeing the breakfast proceedings as the other sparrows gorged on the food kept for them.

Being inquisitive, I left the newspaper and with my favorite cup of Jasmine Tea, went out to the Verandah, to observe quietly. She seemed to be quite in control of the situation as she ensured that all the sparrows got sufficient food. She turned around to greet me with a pleasant "Good Morning!" chirrup.

I wished her back and said. "You seem to be quite experienced at all this."

"Yes," said Mrs. Sparrow, "You see I have children of my own and know how to manage such situations."

Impressed though I was, I couldn't resist asking her, "How do you manage all this along with your hectic life? I mean raising kids, hunting for food, keeping the nest clean, etc?"

"It all goes back to my childhood I guess."

"What do you mean?"

"She looked at the sparrows and fluttered a wing in their direction, "You see I was like them once, a kid. My parents taught me how to be self reliant."

I was surprised at her answer, "Self reliant?" I repeated.

"Yes, we sparrows like other birds, learn at an early age how to fly, search for food, find a suitable partner, and a place to settle down."

"And how do you do that?"

She pecked at a bajra seed and said, "By watching our parents."

"That is indeed plausible, after all you birds do have a sharp vision and as I can see, you are pretty fast, compared to the other birds."

"Yes, we sparrows learn to fly in 2 weeks of hatching and are on our own after another 2 weeks."

"That's amazing!" I couldn't help but exclaim.
I came back into the living room after wishing Mrs. Sparrow a "Pleasant Afternoon!"

After doing my regular holiday chores, throughout the day, I retired for the night.

The next morning also being a holiday, I got up a bit late. Once I settled down again in the living room after spending some time outside, I noticed that a sparrow was trying to fly into the living room, but couldn't as the glass doors were closed.

She would fly close to it and turn back, again fly into it.

This happened several times and as I got up, she was trying to frantically chirrup something to me.

It was Mrs. Sparrow!

"Open up, open up!" she said, desperately approaching the glass door.

Once the door opened, she flew in and sat on the sofa. She appeared a bit out of breath.

"Here, have some water"
I pushed a cup before her after quickly filling it from the kitchen.

After a few moments, I asked her, "What happened?"

She said "I've flown almost 40 Kilometers to meet you. I have a message for you."

"A message for me? Who is it from?" I frowned a little, racking my brains to figure out who would be sending me messages through Mrs. Sparrow.

I didn't have to think too long as Mrs. Sparrow blurted out "From Missy Pigeon."

Mrs. Sparrow's meeting with Missy Pigeon

"Missy Pigeon!?"

The room seemed to reverberate with those two words as I, along with the fish, said it at the same time.

The fish in fact also turned around in unison like synchronized swimmers in a pool to look towards Mrs. Sparrow.

"Where is she"
"How is she?"
"What is she doing?"
"Who did she go with?"
"When is she returning?"
"Why did she go away?"

There were so many questions from all of us, and many more.

Mrs. Sparrow seemed to like the attention that she was getting.

"She's doing fine! She actually went on a pilgrimage"

Perhaps our faces showed question marks all over.

"Yes, on a pilgrimage," repeated Mrs. Sparrow.

We all moved in closer to her to further understand all this. "After all that she had been going through, she decided to go on a pilgrimage." We actually understood what she was saying after she said this for the third time.

"She went to all the major places of worship and meditation centers to find peace, solace and a new meaning to her life. She went to Temples, Churches, Mosques, the Buddhist Pagoda, Fire Temple and even to the nearby Gurudwara.
She would sit inside these places and hear the priests preaching the teachings of the holy books and spend the rest of the

evenings talking with the devotees along with the other birds on the branches of the trees nearby."

"Now that is something!" I couldn't help breaking the silence, the fish were quiet all this while.

"She is fine now" Mrs. Sparrow continued. "In fact, she has started looking at life quite differently and seemed to be quite content with the way things are."

"How did you reach there? The Redcap fish asked

"Actually one of my siblings is a bit spiritually inclined and had been calling me to listen to one of Swamiji's discourses. Only today, when we were talking there, Missy pigeon overheard our address and came to speak with us."

"That's wonderful!" said the Redcap fish.

"She has given her regards to all of you and is looking forward to meeting you again."

"So are we," I said, the fish nodded in approval.

"Thank you friend for this news, you should go and rest now. It must have been a tiring day for you."

As I prepared to draw the curtains and switch off the aquarium light, the sound of flapping wings came again.

"Oh you're back Mrs. Sparrow?"

"Yes!" She said, I forgot to tell you all something."

"OK and what is that?" We were all looking at her

"That Missy Pigeon is getting married next month."

Chapter 10

The Mysterious and Intelligent Crow

He had a very distinct voice. He's always had. The Crow was a bird that was very much there, yet at times never there. He was black, loud (unlike any other bird), unsocial (or believed to be so), and mystical with a fair amount of superstition attached to his being. Almost like the mysterious black cat. He was rarely seen feeding with the other birds and rarely seen at times.

This feathered creature used to come to the window sill once in a while and though he did not seem to be the most pleasant of the lot, he did have a strange attractiveness which none of the other birds had.

He was there when none of the other birds were around. One morning I was able to catch up with him as it ate a chapatti that was kept there.

"Hello there! How are you doing?"

He dropped the chapatti and was about to fly away when I said "Hang on, I just want to talk to you."

Looking a bit confused, he said "Why do you want to talk to me? Everyone else drives me away."

"I am not driving you away, why do you want to fly away?"

He quickly picked up the chapatti, seemed to change his mind, and after dropping it said "I don't trust you Humans."
"I don't blame you, after all Crows are also not very popular with us either." I didn't want to sound rude, but somehow this came out of my mouth.

"Humans are not very popular amongst humans too!" The Crow replied almost in a flash of a second.

"What do you mean?"

"You Humans think that you are the most superior creatures that God ever made, but you are the most stupid."

A Crow saying this to me was a bit disconcerting. However, He had every right to his opinions.

So I quickly said, "And how do you justify that statement?"

"I've been around for some time now and have seen the condition you are in."

"Condition?"

"Yes, You Humans are the cause of your own ruin."

"Can you be a bit specific please?"

"You Humans keep changing with time, you keep getting new things to this world and say that you are developing."

"So, what's wrong with that?"

"You are not happy, you say that you have everything and still you are not happy."

I took a sip of my tea thinking of a reply. The Crow looked at me and said, "And you say that you want to go to heaven."

All this was adding insult to injury, as the Crow, this bird, was getting on my nerves. I still kept my calm as I wanted to hear him out.
"It makes you feel angry when I say all this, doesn't it?" The Crow seemed to see the color of my face change in a second, from white to red and again white.

Of course I was angry even if only for a second as I was trying to digest these words.

The Crow went on, "You just said that Crows are not very popular amongst the Humans, Right?"

"Yes."

"It didn't make me feel angry."

"So?"

"That's why you humans are stupid. You get angry, you get greedy, you get possessive, you fight amongst yourselves, you create your own unhappiness, and then you say that God is not good to you."

All this fell like a bombshell on me, and I had nothing much to do or say, but to finish the tea.

The Crow started pecking on the chapatti again. After much thought, I said..

"Tell me something more about yourself. I would like to get to know you better...."

The Crow looked a bit apprehensive at first, but said, "What do you want to know about me?"

"Anything… where you stay, how you live, what you think. Maybe something about your family, parents etc."

The Crow seemed to be less wary after he probably realized that I truly wanted to talk to him and not shoo him away.

"We are the birds that no one really cares about. People think that we are ugly, yet there is so much more to us that they don't know of."

"Like?" This is just how I had wanted the conversation to go.

"Like we are actually birds that help people. We eat the insects that damage your crop, and also small mice that may be considered pests."

"Yes you are right!"

"We balance nature by cleaning the mess that you humans dump, what you call garbage"

"Hmm that is also right." I agreed to all that the crow was saying.

"And after all the good that we do we get the least respect. I guess life's like that."
The Crow appeared to be dejected. I tried to liven him up and said "Don't feel bad, the world is not always nice to nice people and birds like you, it doesn't mean that you should stop doing all the good work that you've been doing."

"All that is fine, but it's not fair when you are discriminated against in this way. We Crows don't have fine plumage like the other birds, even our voices are raucous, so very different."

After a moment's silence the Crow said again, "It's all because of you humans. You have a very bad habit of discriminating and criticizing others, you never look into your own selves and see your own shortcomings."

The Crow seemingly went on a rant.

"And you think that you are superior to even your fellow human beings. Someone is like this, someone is like that, you have an opinion on everything and everyone but for yourselves." The Crow was really letting off steam.

"Why don't you just accept people, birds and animals the way they are?
Are we also not living beings like you? You just go out and shoot birds and animals for your own greed and fulfillment, because we are helpless against you? Does that make you more powerful than us? Or are you just trying to show that we mean nothing to you? You just want to see things the way it best suites you, disregarding the likes of others. You don't even know how to stay together. Trust me, my father and grandfather and his forefathers said the same thing, that these humans have only been fighting for centuries and they still are today. For what?"

The Crow looked at me. "It's for a reaction" my instincts told me.

Only 2 things came to my mind. First that the Crow was a great orator, and second, he was an even greater actor.

It seemed as though he said what he did to get the response he wanted, quite like a wily politician.

For a second it seemed as though I was standing in a courtroom and the Crow was a lawyer donned in his black attire. He cornered me with his arguments and accusations and I, like the accused stood there searching for words to defend myself. Rather, to defend the entire human race.

After clearing my throat, I said "I think you are over reacting my friend."

Sunil Bhatia

The Crow after looking at me put his eyes down to the ground and walked about 3 feet to my left. He suddenly turned around and then walked in the opposite direction. On reaching the other end he again turned 180 degrees and walked back all the while looking down, with his wings folded behind his back.

He seemed to be in deep thought. Perhaps he was drafting its next little courtroom speech.

"That is your opinion." He said after 3 rounds of pacing on the window sill.

"I am not over reacting, you are too sensitive and a small reaction appears to be an overreaction to you."

"This Crow is brilliant!" I said to myself. "He's even good at creating doubt in my mind about myself."

"You are right," I said to the Crow

"Aha!" he exclaimed. "You are only saying that to please me."

"Well I have to say something to please you because you are pretty displeased at the moment."

The mysterious and intelligent Crow gave a strange grin and started looking at me again.

"And what is the reason for that grin?" This crow was full of surprises

"You have still not answered my question. You digressed from the topic," said the Crow.

"Oh you mean about us being the way we are?" I felt cornered again.

The Crow nodded with a wicked gleam in his eyes.

54

"Oh! That is what you think," I repeated what he had just said to me, giving him a taste of his own medicine.

"I don't just think, but I know," said the Crow.

"Know what?"

"That you humans are basically insecure"

"And what has that got to do with the way we behave?"

"Let me explain," said the Crow. By now he had me in his mental and emotional grip, whether it was intentional or unintentional.

The situation was only how I could counter him. Almost like a tennis player losing his sets and trying to make a comeback.

"You humans depend too much on each other"

"And what is wrong with that?" I was defending myself against this Crow out of all the people.

"That is what makes you insecure," the Crow said calmly.

"That is not insecurity my friend, It is the love and warmth of belongingness that you misinterpret as dependence." I thought I had got even with him.

"Love, warmth, belongingness...yes all is fine. But what happens in the absence of love, warmth and belongingness?"

"This Crow is no angel" I said to myself.

"What are you trying to arrive at?" I countered the Crow.

"All I am trying to say is that you humans are a great species, so long as you are able to find your own happiness, alone."

"My friend, happiness multiplies when it's shared, I hope you agree with this!"

"Yes, but don't tell too many people that you are happy for some may not like it."

"Why?"

"Why? Because it's in the human nature. Not everyone is a true friend who will celebrate your joys and share your pains."

I didn't have much to him, so he continued, "That is why you people are so insecure at times because you run so much after joy, that even a little decline in it makes you uncomfortable."

"Does that mean that I stop enjoying the company of my near and dear ones?" I blurted out.

"No," said the Crow, "It means that you treat happiness and sorrow in a similar manner. Do not be too happy when happy and too sad when sad. Be balanced, and you will find that you will be able to get through life more easily."

"How do you know all this?" These explanations always intrigued me.

"It's because we Crows are linked with you humans, in this life and the life after this."

"How is that possible?" I was flabbergasted by now

"You are forgetting something," the Crow was shaking his head.

"And what is that?"

The Crow looked at the sky, then at me and said, "Your breed feeds us Crows so that the food goes to your ancestors and keeps them happy."

He appeared to be sad after saying this. He knew that I saw him and seemed to understand as well. "You humans are very different," it said.

"What do you mean by that?"

"You never try to do what you want to do." He looked regretfully at me and said "We Crows can see the visible and invisible worlds."

This sounded like Greek to me. I couldn't make a head or tail of what he was saying.

He let out a deep sigh, "You humans want so many things in this world, how many of them do you get?"

"Please be a little specific... sir" I said. This crow deserved respect.

"What do you mean when you say "may his soul rest in peace?"" The crow asked.

"Oh yes, that is a prayer for the departed souls never to come back and have no unfulfilled desires after leaving this earth."

Our conversation seemed to be heading in a completely different direction...but it was ok.

The Crow seemed to be in some deep thought. He finally said, "Do you believe in ghosts or what you call spirits?"

A spooky kind of feeling crept into my veins as I looked around to see if anyone else was nearby. I was, nevertheless, interested in this subject and always had a fascination for the astral sciences. I had read a bit and seen some movies and TV serials on the subject. I had also heard some holy men speak on the same during a religious fair and though outdated to some and perhaps taboo to others, this was indeed something that had caught my attention many a time. This was the chance of a lifetime to get some knowledge, also the Crow was still there and I was not sure if he would stay there for some more time or fly away

"Er... to some extent...what do you know about them?" I acted as if I was not too interested, but in truth was dying to know.

The Crow gave a caw or two as if he was trying to communicate with someone or something.

"Ok, I'll tell you."

At this moment I felt like I was sitting in some kind of a small theater waiting for the play to start and the act to open. In this case it was a one act play, the crow being the only character.

"We Crows have supernatural abilities. We can see both the physical as well as the spirit worlds. We are the messengers who can see the unseen and communicate the same to you"

"I don't understand," is all I could say.

"The spirits come to us crows only, when they want to be lead into the other world. They also try to reach you humans through us."

"Why do they want to communicate with us and why do they come to you?" I was extremely fascinated by now and dropped my act of disinterest.

"There are some souls that are still not liberated."

"Liberated in what sense?" Sometimes I felt that I had too many questions for one life.

"Meaning, these are the souls that are still trapped in the physical world, your world. These are the souls that keep moving around with unfulfilled desires for which they keep trying to return."

All this was highly interesting and worthy of future contemplation. The Crow started cawing again as if he took a little break from our conversation. I realized that I had developed a great reverence for this creature, not to say that the other birds were any less, but he was distinguishingly different. Also because he was, in my opinion a grossly misunderstood bird. Actually being misrepresented and associated with anything and everything that is apart from good.

"What were you cawing right now?"

"Our voices are generally indicators of change. A few people say that when we are around, something magical will happen."

"Why do the spirits come to you?"

"Because they can only be seen and heard by us." He gave a faint smile.

"And what do they tell you?"

"Oh lots of things like 'can you tell my children that I still love them?', or 'just tell my friend that I miss him a lot'. You know the usual."

By now quite a few things started falling in perspective.

"May I offer you something more to eat?" I noticed that the chapatti that the crow had been pecking on intermittently was now over.

"A little water is fine," said the crow.

After having had some water, he said that he had to leave, but before that he said, "I have something to tell you."

"What?"

"It's actually a secret."

"Yes please tell me." This was like a bonus for me considering the fact that the Crow was about to leave.

"What would you say if I told you that we may never meet again?"

I was too dumbstruck by this statement. I found it hard to accept it.

"Why do you say that? You live around this place right? We can always meet again."

"The fact is that we Crows have a mission. There is a reason for our existence."
There was silence for some time, and on seeing that I had nothing to say, the Crow continued.

"We are the carriers of the lost souls, the guides to those still reeling in darkness, to take them and to set them free into the realm of light."

I let out a sigh.

"We set these anguished souls free from the chains of their past lives and take them to higher worlds of self knowledge. We even teach things to living beings like you."

"And what is that?"

"The next time a Crow is near you, know that some change going to happen in your life. We try to take you to a new level of consciousness, and self acceptance by telling you to let go of old beliefs and the emotional pain of the past. There is no point in having this suffering for there is a better life if we learn to forgive people who have hurt us."

"Tell me something more" I said feebly. I knew I was pushing my luck as the crow was ready to fly off.

"We crows are the keepers of the higher orders of right and wrong and also the guardians of ceremonial magic and healing. We are the embodiment of truth and that is why many people don't like us, but let me tell you that our harsh voices bring balance and harmony, for it brings people like you back to reality as you humans have a habit of dwelling in illusion."

I was rendered speechless.

"We live beyond the realm of space and time and even help you humans to look into yourselves, see the dark shadows and also the light within, so that you are able to set yourselves free."

"But why can't we meet again?" I definitely sounded a bit desperate.

"Because I follow the spirits and they also follow me. Our meeting was by chance and can happen once again in this world, or the afterworld."

"Sir it has been a great honor for me to have met you."

"I have to go now. Thanks for the water."

He flew up and vanished in a tree nearby. A breeze started blowing which swayed the flora around. Many Crows started cawing all of a sudden and it broke the silence.

I was left there alone and all I could say was "Thank you friend! Hope we meet again."

Chapter 11

The Song of the Nightingale

Sometime, at the start of Summer, I remember that I was staying in office till late, trying to reply to clients, as the workload had increased. By the time I reached home and had dinner, after watching a bit of TV or chatting online with my friends, it would easily be around 2 AM. This was beginning to become a habit.

This was the time when Crow sounds used to come and by that time would I would be tucked up in bed as had to get up the next morning for work.

Once it so happened that as the next day was a holiday, I stayed awake for some more time.
It was 3 am and when it was quiet as ever, a beautiful sound filled the air.

At first I thought that it was some kind of doorbell belonging to a neighbor or the sirens that are sometimes put in cars while they backed. Wave after wave this sound rose in the air with such precision and melody that it was quite baffling. I decided to step out and investigate the same, forgetting whatever else it was that I was doing.

As I searched under the night lamps one by one to detect the source of this sound, the security guard approached me and said "Aap kya dhundh rahein hain?" (What are you searching for?)

Since I couldn't think of anything else, I simply asked him "Ye awaz kahan se aa rahi hai?"(Where is this sound coming from?)

He pointed to a tree in the other direction. As I made my way there, the sound continued to emanate through the night and this was surely something that I was not going to leave. I searched from leaf to leaf trying to find a trace, a moving object, a swaying branch ...anything.

Since the volume had increased, I deduced that I was quite close to whatever I was looking for. Finally with still no trace of the source, I just started calling out softly..

"Hello... Hello?"

There was no response. The sound continued, so I tried again, "Hello? Can you hear me, what's your name?"

The sound stopped abruptly and finally I got a reply, "I am the Nightingale!"

I heaved a sigh of relief and spoke out, "I want to talk to you"

Within seconds a small creature appeared out of the darkness and sat on a twig right in front of me.

"I must compliment your singing, why have you chosen this odd hour for your recital?"

"It's odd for you, not for us nightingales."

"Yes, I suppose, what you say is true. After all we all are different."

She almost immediately replied, "I would beg to differ on that."

"Really? How come?"

"Do you know that we also sing by day?"

"Well, no. I haven't actually heard your voice in the day time."

"That's because in the day, there's so much noise.."

After some moments of silence, I said "You are right...but that's normal isn't it? We humans are awake in the day and need to move around for our livelihood, meet people and need to do so much more."

"We nightingales are also awake at that time. We need to alert each other of our territories, mate, reach out to our fellow birds and amidst all the noise, we still manage to sing louder."

"But how are you like us humans?"

"What is the most important thing in life?"

This was quite a bit of a stunner from this little winged friend, much less expected.

"The most important thing if you look at basics is to have food, clothing and shelter."

"Does every human being have that?"

I was trying to figure out what she was trying to arrive at.

"No."

Then she dropped one more question which kind of caught me by surprise..

"What causes you human beings the most sorrow? Think about it."

I had no immediate answer to that and finally said "There are many things that cause us sorrow, I really don't know what to talk about. I guess different people will have different answers to both your questions."

The nightingale gave an interesting look "You humans think that you are different from each other but I can say that you are not"

I had no choice but to ask the nightingale

"So what are the answers to both your questions?"

The night had become quite still by now. Even the breeze stopped and there wasn't even the rustle of a leaf. It was just me and the nightingale and the two questions which had been put before me.

"So?" I urged the Nightingale. Of course I was curious to know what she would say.

"What is the most important thing in life?"

The nightingale said, "I had said something about us singing in the daytime sometime back"

"Yes" I said, "And I had mentioned that you couldn't be heard. You said it's because of the noise."

"After that I had also said something else."

I tried to recall, then it came to my mind "Yes you said that you sing louder but, I still can't figure out what your answer is"

"Dear fellow, you should have known by now."

"I can make a few guesses, but I know that it may not be the right answer."

"I must say that we are having a fine conversation," the nightingale let out a small sound which I thought may have been her version of a chuckle.

After this she started singing again it was the same sound which had pulled me out.

I did not have the heart to interrupt her as she seemed to be enjoying every moment of it. The best thing was that she sang in two different pitches, yet they seemed to be in the right pattern.

As I stood there in awe of this wonderful moment, the early rays of sunlight started breaking the still of the night.

The performance seemed to go on eternally as if the nightingale had totally forgotten me. Perhaps she had and it was ok with me, for in that state she sang even more beautifully.

She finally stopped and turned around to look at me as if she had expected me to be there.

"So?" I again asked the same question.

She took a deep breath, and happily replied, "The most important thing in life is to be heard."

I was quite impressed by her reply, but couldn't help asking, "What do you think is the reason for our existence?"

What a question to ask!!! I really didn't know what had prompted me to ask that.

"Well one reason is to find out the answer to that question." It was quite a smart answer from her.

"But that's why I'm asking you, do you know the answer?"
"Suppose if you know the answer eventually, would it make any difference to your life?"

We just seemed to be tossing questions at each other.

"Yes it would bring a great deal of satisfaction, for it would be the end of the search"

For that you would have to go to the second question that I asked you."

"What causes us humans the most sorrow?" I repeated the question.

"Yes, you know the answer." The nightingale became quiet after that and looked at me.

This was getting deeper and deeper..yet I seemed to be still on the surface.

I started remembering many things, different times and situations that had crossed my life, the joys and sorrows. The realization hit me that they all seemed to come and go for smaller or larger periods of time.

Many things came together and a larger seemingly immeasurable amount of emotion started building up: joy, exhilaration, anger, sadness, as different experiences from the past filled my mind.

"You just said that the most important thing in life is to be heard."

"That's right." the nightingale spoke out

"So I guess what causes the most sorrow is when people don't listen to you."

"Well you're pretty close, but I must say that you humans give too much importance to too many things in life, especially to what others say or how they feel about you."

That put me in a slightly contemplative mood.

"What do you have to say about people who just love their quiet world. You know there are some people who just don't want to be heard?"

"What you say is right," said the Nightingale. Even those people when alone are hearing something which wants to be heard."

"And what is that?"

"It's the voice of their consciousness."

The chirruping of morning birds seemed to slowly fill the air as dawn approached.

"You seem to know a lot," I said to the nightingale.

"Oh! I don't know a lot. I just know what is required not what is not required."

"And how do you know what is required and what is not?"

"I am very focused you see, we don't believe in wasting any time."

My eyebrows shot up in surprise and curiosity. It went on, "We have to catch insects, take care of our territories, make our nests and even teach our little ones how to sing. It's very important for us to use our time wisely"

It almost seemed that I was attending a time management class. A thought suddenly came to me, "Tell me, don't you ever make mistakes? We human beings in fact spend a lot of time in this activity itself."

The nightingale looked at me for a few seconds and said, "We do, but we learn quickly, move on and don't repeat those mistakes again. We understand the value of time."

"Wow!!" I thought to myself, "One can learn a lot from this tiny little bird."

"Opportunity is the biggest thing you see, we can see our worms and know when to catch them." These words still reverberate in my mind.

"What if there are no worms?" This was expected to come from me.

"There will always be worms, you just have to find them. If you don't find an opportunity, you have to make it or go on to the next one.!!!"

"How do you do that?"

"We nightingales also face situations. The simplest one being loud traffic noise..."

"What's that got to do with the opportunity?"

"We sing louder so that we can communicate with each other to stay safe from predatory birds and also to find our worms and insects"

"Yes in our lives too we humans have to overcome obstructions also...you never answered Qn.2?"

"Yes, OK.. what causes most unhappiness is when we are unable to hear our own inner voice..once we hear it, it's then that we find ourselves once again and tranquility returns.."

By now the sun was faintly visible over the horizon. As I got ready to leave, I complimented the nightingale on her time management skills and also her knowledge and wisdom.

"So...we'll catch up again?"

The nightingale said "Perhaps a few times till this year end."

"Why? Are you migrating somewhere next year?"

"No!" She said.

"We nightingales live for around 2 years and I'm already a year and a half old…"

Chapter 12

A Special Afternoon

One Sunday afternoon Missy Pigeon got married.

All the neighboring birds were invited to the parapet of my balcony. Missy Pigeon wanted to have it there due to 'sentimental' reasons as it's there that she had spent a good amount of her time.

The fish were overjoyed and the excitement grew as everyone was eager to see the groom. Though the fish could not come out of the aquarium, I had moved the curtains and sofa aside for them to get a clearer view of the outside.

After much waiting he arrived and flew down to sit next to Missy Pigeon.
It was Mr. Pigeon.

All the fish were dumbfounded, as the Red Cap fish smiled. Her predictions had come true. Missy Pigeon did get him in the end. More than anything else, they were surprised to know, especially the goldfish that Missy Pigeon had forgiven him after he begged for her friendship again. He promised never to leave her again for any other Pigeon and had realized all she had gone through because of him.

All the other birds said that she was genuinely a good hearted pigeon and this act on her part would go a long way as an example in the bird community.

"So you did it!" I told Missy Pigeon with a grin.

"Actually you may say that it was meant to happen this way. That's the funny thing about life, the more you long for something, the more difficult it seems to get. The moment you forget about it, it doesn't really matter whether you get it or not, but yes I'm really very happy that it turned out this way."

Missy Pigeon also thanked the Red Cap fish for her timely help and said that she would keep visiting us whenever she was able to. The couple had decided to stay in the Garden on the other side of the block for the summers and as per their new understanding, Missy Pigeon agreed to move over to the high rise building for some period of time which Mr. Pigeon liked.

"Marriage is all about understanding your partner you see" She said. "We both have to keep each other happy."

Thus ended the story of Missy Pigeon and once they flew away, I turned to the Red cap fish and asked her, "How on earth did you know that he would come back to her?"

She beckoned me to come closer as she said "I only prayed that he'd come back and wished that she'd be with him."

"So you were not sure yourself?"

"Life is quite a bit of a puzzle my friend. We don't know what turn it will take. I was also prepared for the fact that Mr. Pigeon would not return."

"Then why did you give Missy Pigeon so much of hope?"

"Because it gave her the strength to keep moving on with her life."

I had a good night's sleep that night and woke up on time for work the next morning. I was not particularly fond of Mondays. But for the first time I somehow looked forward to the day...

Chapter 13

The Peacock Family

There was great excitement in the aquarium.

I had gotten some new fish food and they were loving it.

"You should take better care of your own food too" said one of the Goldfish. "You've been eating at midnight of late."

I was in a hurry a usual, running after time and while locking the door waved a quick bye to the finned creatures.

The next day was a Sunday and outings on an off day had become common of late. Earlier I was content being at home, doing some reading, watching T.V., listening to music, but these days I wanted to do something different.

I found myself close to some nice gardens as I wandered across the city that afternoon with nothing else to do. To my surprise, I saw a Peacock near some fountains. Very soon he started displaying his tail spread out like a fan. The Peahen, who was probably his wife, stood nearby and watched the spectacle.

As she walked up to me, I told her "Very Beautiful," pointing to the
Peacock, "He really has gorgeous plumage."

The Peahen looked knowingly in the direction and said "Yes of course! Every bird can't be as good looking as us, we are after all Peacocks!"

"Uh oh!" I thought to myself "So we have this in birds also."
The Peahen then proudly introduced her baby, "Here's junior, doesn't he look marvelous?"

"Yes he does."

"And here comes my husband, the Peacock"

He struck a pose, stood for a moment then walked across the lawn towards us with his tail sweeping behind him like a bridal train.

It was the area around the Governor's house and so this glimpse of royalty seemed natural.

I took a round of the area, had a look around of the coast as the bunglow was on the seaside. After an hour or so I decided to return home.

I just thought of seeing off the peacock family once more on my way out. As I came near the garden, the Peahen came running towards me. She looked distressed.

"Have you been near this place? Where were you?"

"I just went nearby for a bite. What happened?

The Peahen almost broke down. "Junior's missing! He just disappeared!"

The Peacock Family & The Hunt for Junior

The police gathered all around in a very short span of time, after all the incident happened near the Governor's Bungalow.

The Peahen was devastated and as she sobbed before me, the Peacock came near us. Almost out of nowhere a tiff started, "You never took care of Junior. All you did was glide around and show off your feathers. Only we moms know what we have to go through to raise our babies."

The Peacock looked a bit shaken by whatever had happened but tried to show that he was taking it in his stride. He tried to console his wife but she just went on, "He's our only child..."

I felt moved at her plight and tried to make some headway in this case as I popped in a chewing gum. Apparently chewing gum made me think clearly.

"I would say that since this is rather a serious matter, I am sure the local authorities are going to go all out. Peacocks are a highly valued species of bird. Let's start by first trying to remember where and when you last saw Junior."

All that the Peahen remembered was that he was playing near the lawn fence half an hour ago. A few people nearby were interrogated by the police but no one was really bothered.

"Are you going to do something about it?" the Peahen demanded from the Peacock.
"I am sure the police will look into this matter" he said. "As it is we can't leave this place..also I have some foreign dignitaries visiting the governor tomorrow so have to put up a show again."

"You are simply impossible!" the Peahen cried out in desperation as she glared at him.

I wanted to console her and said, "Let's hope for the best. I'm sure we'll get to the bottom of this matter and will hear about your son in a day or two." I was just trying to bring some consolation to the Pea hen. But it did seem strange, how junior was there one moment and then not to be seen the next."

There was a flapping sound from a nearby tree and I saw a slightly larger bird come near us. He came and sat on the fence and through the growing darkness I could still see that it was a vulture. In fact an old vulture, weathered over time with ruffled feathers and weary look on his face.

As we looked at him not knowing how to react, he gave a grunt and said in a deep hoarse tone, "Children, I believe that you are looking for a baby peacock. I saw a man carrying it off an hour ago in that direction." He waved a wing slightly to our right towards a road going eastwards.

Chapter 14

The Jolly Old Vulture

This came as a blessing in disguise. The Peahen got very excited at the revelation that at least someone knew what happened to her child.

"When did you see them?"

"About an hour ago."

"Are you sure?" I intervened

"I'm old, but my eyesight is still good" the old Vulture said with an air of affirmation.

"How can you be so sure?" I asked again.

The old Vulture came near us and said, "Look children, I live on that tree from where I came right now, people don't know that but I see a lot of things that go on around here"

"But I've never seen you here" The Peahen exclaimed.

"That's because I don't come out in the day. We Vultures are not looked upon with great fondness you see."

"But you can fly wherever you want to. Right?"

The Vulture gave a grunt again and said "Well, I am old now."

We looked at him hoping to hear something more.

"Yes I have flown to great heights in my younger days, all the other birds had a lot of regard for me then, but I am old now and can't fly much."

"How can you be sure that you saw my Junior only?" The Peahen was really worked up.

"I see you all every day. Besides yours is the only Peacock family in this area."
"How can I trust that... that you have not taken junior away?" The Peahen was clearly hyper by now. It however set me thinking along those lines.

"I do not blame you for the way you are thinking, but I have nothing to give you other than my assurance that I have nothing to do with your child's disappearance."

The Peahen started sobbing. There was very little that could be done at this point of time, and the old vulture seemed to be the only ray of hope if he was telling the truth.
"You stole my baby!" The Peahen burst out inconsolably, "You must have eaten him by now!"

It was a bit of a fix but the Old Vulture kept his calm. "If there is any way in which I can get the little peacock back, I will do so, perhaps then you would believe in me."

It was late and I had to reach home so I left. I got busy from the next day and the entire week kept relentlessly piling work on

Sunil Bhatia

me. I was exhausted by the weekend, so I took another trip on Saturday evening to see the Peacock family.

The Peahen looked a little pale and ushered me close to her as soon as she saw me.

"Any luck?" I asked hopefully.

"No! The Vulture has given some information. His relatives further saw a man with my child almost ten miles away."

"Let me speak with him" I got up and went near the tree where he stayed. He was there and said that he was happy to see me.

"This younger generation is very restless, I must say." He started speaking out with a shaking head. I have been telling the Peahen to be a little patient but all she does is get worked up, I tell you it's affecting her health."

"You must have seen a great deal in your time."

"What to say," coughed the Vulture, "You can say that am now at the brink of my existence."
He started cackling in amusement.

"Maybe you can teach me a thing or two about life." I was getting to my favorite pass time again.

"What do you want to know?"

"Anything about life."

"Aah life…" The Vulture smiled at me.

"Why are you smiling?"

"Because you asked about life"

"Ok?"

80

"Life my friend is meant to be lived, each and every moment, and felt each and every moment. That's what makes it so fulfilling"

I quietly took this in and then said, "Tell me more!"
He gave a little cough and said
"I have gone through a great till now, that's what has made me what I am today!" He suddenly started laughing.

"What's so funny?"

"I'm laughing at all the times that I went through, when I didn't know a thing about what to do, what a fool I made of myself!"

"And it makes you laugh?" I said sheepishly.

"Yes it does, when I think of how I reacted in those times."

"You must have been a child then."

"Yes" chuckled the vulture, "I was a child then and I still am one now! The other birds think that I'm crazy but they have all grown old with their thoughts."

"Grown old with their thoughts"...that sounded new.

"Please explain what you meant by that"

"Oh, do you know that our thoughts shape our lives? I learnt that a long time ago."

"But you can't feel happy and optimistic all the time, can you? "I was in my usual questioning mood.

The Vulture again burst out laughing.

"You laugh again...!" This provoked my curiosity further.

After he stopped, his eyes started glowing much like a mischievous child as he looked at me. They seemed to be full of life.

"Wait a minute," I thought to myself, "Full of life. That explains it all."

"Are you always like this?" I asked the Vulture.

"What's wrong with it?" The Vulture was still grinning.

"Err.. Well.." I didn't seem to have a reply. I realized that everyone was different.

"My friend, life is full of many experiences. Don't you think that we would be able to face them better if we take life sportingly?"

This was valuable education from a Vulture. However I was not convinced.

"When life is not always fair how can one be jovial?" I shot back at him.

"Yes, life is not always fair, but it never stops giving you chances and taking them is entirely in your hands."

A winged creature was telling this to a human being.

"But one can't be happy all the time." I argued.

"Why not?"

"Because its so..so.. Childish and stupid.."

"In that case, you are in the company of a childish and stupid bird"

"But you are not that way!!!"

82

"You only said it!"

"I'm sorry, didn't mean to offend you.." I really hoped the vulture didn't feel bad.

The Jolly Old Vulture and the unbelievable

"Oh..it's alright I know why people say what they say, so it doesn't bother me at all."

"What kind of a bird is this?" I thought to myself. "He doesn't even feel bad when someone else could get touchy..."

"You must be totally out of your mind" Again I thought that I had sounded rude.

"I was never in it" The vulture burst out laughing again. "You see most of the times we are living in someone else's mind."

Now what was that supposed to mean? I gave the Vulture a blank look.

The Vulture could see the confusion on my face and responded "In simple terms it means that our minds are more interested in controlling others' minds. Such is the nature of the mind that it seeks its freedom and so it begins to wander and since it is able to connect with other minds it tries at some point of time to overpower the other mind and take that space."

By now was thoroughly confused. The Vulture looked amused at my reactions and said, "Let's change the topic. I almost forgot to tell you that one of my distant cousins is coming shortly to visit me."

"Oh that's great! Will say hello to him incase he comes soon, as I have to get back.

No sooner than I had said this, than a draft of air brushed against my face and another bird came and sat next to the Vulture.

"Oh so you've arrived!" The Vulture said joyously.

He kept a wing on the visitor, turned towards me and said, "Meet my cousin.
I was just telling you about him."

The visitor looked at me and said, "Hello...how are you doing?"

The visitor looked familiar. It was almost like in a state of being hit by a thunderbolt in the seconds thereafter as a memory flashed in my mind!

Y.y.youare the...? I stammered and couldn't speak at all after that.

"Yes" It said, "You are right!"

He was the Falcon from the strange dream that I had had a few months ago..

Chapter 15

The Mystical Falcon

"So you've met before," The Vulture chuckled and looked at the Falcon. "He has a way of reaching out to others..ha ha!" The vulture then stretched his wings and yawned. "I need to get some sleep now. Age permits me to stay awake no longer. See you tomorrow." With that the Old Vulture vanished in the branches above and left me alone with the Falcon.

Still unable to believe my eyes, I finally asked.. "How did you come in that strange dream which I had a few months ago? And.. and now you appear like this before me?"

The Falcon gave the same profound look as he had done in the dream and said, "I told you then also that your life is the dream and this is for real."

All this seemed so intriguing just like the dream had been

"Ok, ok... for a second let me believe in what you're saying, just please tell me how you came here when you were there."

The Falcon smiled and said, "The same way you are here and reached there."

By now I was totally lost and left groping for some sense.

"All I know is that this is my reality, and you can't change that." I managed to say this with a fair amount of conviction.

"Ok!" The Falcon finally agreed or so I thought heaving a sigh of relief.

"But there is a time at least once a day when this reality of yours is not with you." The Falcon was absolutely still. Only his voice floated through the darkness.

"All right," maybe I was beginning to give in a bit, but I was still ready for a battle of wits. "And when is that?"

The Falcon was still motionless and said "When you are asleep."

I thought for a moment, then said, "So how come you are here today?"

"My distant cousin the Vulture called me to help in finding the baby peacock."

"What's your take on it?" I somehow knew that the Falcon would have a convincing answer.

"The little fellow is safe. As of now, it seems that they can't find him"

"Where do you think he is?"

"Well, all I know right now is that he's safe and alive, as you are aware I have just arrived."
"How can you be so sure?"

"We Falcons can see all what happens in the heavens, on earth and below"

"Below?"

"There are more worlds than just this one my friend."

It took a moment for me to absorb this. It was pretty late in the night and thankfully no souls around. Otherwise I would have been labeled crazy being all alone there at that time of the night. No sooner did this came to my mind, than the Falcon said..

"There are quite a few..."

"What?" Startled I asked.

"Souls" said the Falcon. There are quite a few of them around, and you may be considered crazy for being here at this time of the night but you are not."

The Falcon had read my thoughts.

"How did you do that? How could you just read my thoughts?"

"My friend," The Falcon gave the same knowing look, "You are forgetting that you are with me."

"So?"

"We are not different you see.'

"You're kidding me! You're a bird and I'm a human being."
"In form, yes." The Falcon gave a smile for the first time.

"Ok you win but you still haven't answered my question."

"Our thoughts are not different, because we are not different." The Falcon paused after that. "We are actually the same."

I was not sure whether to laugh or feel exasperated at this while the Falcon continued, "So what you think is audible to me."

"Ah! Then why don't I hear what you think?" Victory was on my side in that argument.

"Because I don't think, I only experience" The Falcon had once again given a feasible, if not convincing answer.

I just looked at the falcon and said, "You come in my dreams, you come in my life, you read my thoughts…What else can you do?"

"I have come here to find the baby peacock on the insistence of my cousin, I will consider doing that for the time being."

As usual I had spent too much time and had to leave for home but I still said, "I would like to ask one question."

"Go ahead."

I somehow felt that the Falcon knew what the question was but still asked, "Can you see the future? I would like to know a few things about myself."

The Falcon looked at me for a second then said, "You already know."

I was lost for a moment "You need not ask me that. You know what you want, and also know how to get it. It's all within you."

With steps leading the way to home, I finally reached my place, still in a daze and went off to sleep.

Chapter 16

The Lively Duck

A few days after the missing baby peacock incident, I found myself near a Duck that was to teach me a lesson...

This was a noisy Duck and between the loud sounds which the other ducks made, this particular duck was the noisiest. Any bystander would have taken a gun and shot it down as a disrupter of the peace and serenity of the neighborhood, but luckily this had not happened.

Not surprisingly, I was next to her in no time and the particularly loud Duck was gracious enough to reward me with her silence, for some time at least.

"Don't you think you are a nuisance? You are awfully loud I must say."

She looked amused. I finally had to ask it, "So why have you become like this?"

She was still quiet. She seemed to be laughing inside and finally said, "You humans will never learn."

"Wait a second, you are the one that was making such a ruckus."

Was I complaining?

She came near me and sat down. She was still quiet.

"And what do you expect me to say now?"

Was I seething inside?

"I never said anything, it's you who's doing all the talking."

She still seemed to be rejoicing inside

"Why have you become so quiet now?"

Little did I realize that the Duck was enjoying every moment of this conversation

"Say something!" This seemed to unnerve the Duck.

All the other Ducks had moved on by now. She looked up and finally after what seemed a lifetime, said, "You humans beings will never learn. Why are you like this?"

"Like what?" I was reaching the edge of my patience.

"You are always critical of everything, finding fault with everyone and everything around you."

Knowing that I would not have an answer to this the Duck continued,

"Can't you ever let things be the way they are? Is it necessary to change everything?"

I calmed myself down and after a while said, "You seem to be offended. Is it because I complained about your being noisy?"

The duck shot back almost instantaneously

"Stop pointing fingers at me. No one's perfect and neither are you!"

Cut down to size, I gave a very penitent look at the Duck.

She suddenly started quacking loudly again. It was after a few quacks that I realized that they were in glee. The Duck was having a good laugh!
"Don't be so serious my friend, It seems that I got you."

"Yes you did, but you are right! You have to also agree that you were being noisy."

"What you call noise is the way we are. We need to communicate with each other.
We are born this way."

That set me thinking, 'Born this way'. How nice it would have been had we to live the way we are.

"Why should we change the way we are?" The Duck was all out to prove her point.

Carefully choosing my words I said, "Yes, we should not change ourselves, but it works differently with us human beings." I had begun sounding a little dejected after having said this.

She gave me a hard look and as she analyzed the situation, she came closer to me. "You know you really don't need to change yourself." Was she trying to console me?

"But we have to, otherwise we would not be accepted. That's how it goes with us."

She again broke into her laughter quacks and after many of them said

"Let me tell you something."

The Lesson from the lively duck

"I have been studying you humans for a while now. You people change with time."

I was taken aback, by her observation.

"Of course we do my friend. Otherwise we won't be able to survive."

"We ducks, like any other bird, never try to change ourselves. There's really no need to do so."

"You make it sound so simple" I said, "It's not that easy for us humans, we need to change, otherwise we won't progress in life."

"Aah yes... Progress" The duck was trying to get at something and started quietly contemplating.

"What's wrong with that? Yes we try changing our ways for the better." I had to defend myself.

"Yes and in the bargain, you change yourselves." The duck murmured. "There is no need for that really" she concluded.

I looked at her quietly, so she continued, "Let me ask you a question, do you like changing yourself, rather do you like it when you have to change yourself just because people tell you to do so?"

After some thought, I sai, "Well, to tell the truth, no! It's really tough to do things just because you are told to do so. One tends to lose one's original self."

"Ahaa! I was expecting that reply" She broke out with a happy look on her face. "And still you do it and keep on doing it again and again."

"If we don't, the others will learn newer things and leave us far behind." This seemed to be the only logical answer at this point of time.

"Hmm... I now understand how you guys think." The duck almost became motionless for a moment... then said, "But tell you what, you still don't need to change yourself. The moment you change yourself, you lose yourself!"

Something hit me in the brain. I just let all this talk seep in. The Duck sure knew a thing or two about us and seemed to be hell bent to put her point across.

"You seem to be talking sense my friend, but it's not practical" What else could I say?

"Your practical life doesn't make sense to us birds" She sounded very sure "You've got it all wrong. You are going against nature."

"We need to control nature otherwise nature would control us." I countered.

"Ahaa, control...you just said it."

"What's wrong with that? We can't let winds blow us away, rivers flood our streets. We do need to control nature."

"And that includes other human beings that are part of nature."

"Well..." I got stuck there for a moment.

"That's the whole thing, why can't you just let life be?" She seemed to be right.

"That's not possible. We need to move in the direction that we feel is right."

After a few moments of silence the Duck said, "The moment you change yourself, you lose yourself!"

I could see what the Duck was driving at.

"And you try to change too many things; you will forget who you are."

"Change is necessary for the better." This had to be right from what I had learnt.

"Then it is not change. What you see as change is surely not for the better, for if it is not in harmony with nature, it is not change"

I could not understand that, so asked, "How do you manage not to change?"
I wanted the Duck to defend herself now.

"You must have heard of an old saying, try throwing water on a Duck's back"

She started to smile.

Chapter 17

The Lonely Bat

It was a full moon night. I was unable to sleep as the silvery light kept pouring through the window shades. A strange screeching sound kept emanating from the night followed by such sounds.

I got up. After seeing that it was around 3 am, I went out on the balcony. The full moon was stunningly beautiful.

The screeching sound continued till a flapping windy sensation came close. I was still not able to gauge which creature this was. After much waiting it came nearby again and after many flaps, it vanished into thin air. I went back to the bedroom and tried to go back to sleep. The sound carried on for a while and then a little squeaky sound seemed to enter my mind.

"What you seek, is what you shall find."

I got up suddenly not able to understand where this voice was coming from and thought I must have dreamt it.

I tried going to sleep, again after a few minutes the same voice came in my head again.

"You're wasting your time."

I was truly awake now, though unable to understand what was going on. After drinking some some water, I made a valiant effort again to go back to sleep.

The silvery moonlight played hide and seek as the breeze kept moving the window shades. I went into a faint dream imagining a strange creature that was part monkey, part bird, part human being. I had never seen anything like him before. He seemed to fly freely through the night with great precision and with not one but many such birds.

This bird had magical powers as he flew around turning all it touched into gold. There were people who worshipped him and held him in high regard.

It was a strange thing that the dream just went on despite this bird not being one of the most beautiful sights that I had come across.

The bird kept appearing and vanishing, then appearing again. After flying around in my dreams, he came right in front and hung upside down on an empty wooden wall hook. My eyes opened and I saw it there.

"Who's there?"

"I'm a bat..." The squeaky voice resonated through the darkness.

It took me a few seconds to adjust to the moonlit night.
Finally saw the creature which was hanging upside down. It was indeed a very unique sight.

"You seem to be different to the others"

"Yes, I'm a bat"

"Why are you hanging upside down?"

"Everything is not always as you believe it to be"

I reflected a bit, "Yes, but you are different. What brings you here?"

The bat looked at me for a few seconds and then said, "I prefer being alone at times, we are a somewhat lonely species. Actually I came here to tell you something."

"Tell me what?"

"Something had been on your mind for a while." He said.

"Yes, a lot of things actually, but that's life isn't it?" I replied.

"Agreed, but there is something that you've been thinking of lately, more than anything else."

I finally gave up, "Yes, can you do something about it?"

The bat seemed to go into deep meditation with his eyes closed.

He responded after a few moments and said, "You have to release yourself."

"From what?" I said. Not quite getting it.

"Yes" said the bat his eyes still closed.

"You are not what you should be, and to be that, you have to go into your past."

I was fully awake now, and switched on the table lamp and could clearly see the bat.

"You are carrying too much of your past with you" The bat spoke in a clearer squeak. "You tend to worry at times about the future. You have to get released."

Sunil Bhatia

By now the bat had my full attention.

"What do you mean?"

The bat suddenly flew off the hook and vanished through the window, into the night.

"Hey, where are you going?" I called out.

I got up and looked out of the window. The beautiful full moon was still there. The same squeaky voice again spoke in my head..

"You have to get released, now go to sleep."

I started feeling drowsy. The bat appeared in my dreams. He seemed to be communicating quite clearly through the haze that was there. Of all the experiences that I had had with my feathered friends, this one seemed to be the most intriguing. I was dreaming but was yet in my senses.

He seemed to be filling my mind with strange lights, silver, golden, violet. Patches of colors seemed to appear and fade again and again.

"What are you doing?" I asked.

There was no reply. I only heard a squeak or two.

Then I had visions of strange caves with carved faces. I drifted through the arches of an old building and heard the sounds of people talking, children playing and then… Silence.

Complete silence followed by pitch black darkness. Then the sounds began. This time gurgling rivers and windy skies.

The bat spoke, "You are now in your being. Tell me what you see and how you feel."

98

"This is strange..these places seem familiar." I said to the bat.

"Ah, I thought so. What do you make out of all this?"

"I... I don't know." All this was strangely exciting, almost like a mystery novel

"You have to be released." The squeaky voice filled my mind with an echo.

I felt like I was in the middle of nowhere, as light kept coming and going.

"Where are you bat? Have you left me?" I asked as the light continued to play with the darkness.

"Now go... go to the places where you have been before." The bat spoke again.

I floated up to the sky in an instance and moved around freely. A sudden rush of sights crossed my mind. People, places, words said, things done.

All of a sudden the bat spoke again, "Go.. The time is short and I have to leave."

I walked around the old building which was empty. I heard the sound of a baby crying. I went closer to the door from where it was coming. The door, all of a sudden, changed into a cave wall, the same one I had seen a short while ago.

And then, there was a face that I knew. It was my mom in her youth entering into this cave with flowers in her hands.

No sooner did I reach close to her, than she looked in the direction from where I was approaching and then she gave a gentle smile.

I could see her but it appeared as if she could only sense my being.

'My being'! That's what the bat just said some time ago, "You are now in your being."

The caves vanished and I was near the door again.

I saw a lady's back and a child in her arms as she was trying to console it. I was in front of them in no time... It was my mom again !

I took a look at the child... It had to be my elder brother or sister. I was not quite able to figure out why I was there, when mom again looked in my direction.

I was stunned to see that the baby was me. This was the same child whose pictures were in our family photo albums, taken when I was born.

"How do you feel? The bats voice filled my mind."

"I can't say. Why am I here? All this is so strange."

The bat gave a squeaky laugh and said, "Why do you question so much?"

"Why shouldn't I?"

"Because you are ignoring how you feel at that point of time."

I became quite after that and the bat went on, "Just go with the feeling, don't question and you will open your senses to the wonder that surrounds you."

I felt a cool breeze on my face and there was darkness again. The bats image slowly appeared again. He said "How do you feel now?"

"I don't know. Why is all this happening?"

"Another question." The bat gave a funny squeak. And then he pinned me with an intense gaze and said "You have certain patterns in your being that need to go."

I could feel a strange energy around me.

"That's it! I am able to see it now!" It said excitedly.

The bat descended through the darkness and sat down right before me.

The teachings of the Bat.

"What can you see?" I curiously inquired. "Are you able to read my face?" I added.

"We bats cannot see the physical world, as you might know we are blind."

I was dumbstruck by this revelation. Yes, I remembered that bats used sound waves to travel.

"What do you see?" I repeated again, a bit impatiently.

"I see your past lives and your unseen secrets my friend."

"My what?" This was not entirely Greek for me but extremely fascinating.

"Remove the word 'My' from your words, it blocks your transition."

The bat had become like a therapist, I was totally lost within his mystic ways.

"Aah, so your heart has many secrets, and mind with many thoughts that are buried deep down inside."

"None that I am aware of," All this while I was experiencing strange sensations.

"The darkness that you dwell in will show you the light that you have been seeking." As the bat spoke, I slipped into an immense infinite space, almost in a tizzy, yet all this seemed to bring some sort of comfort. As the bat had said earlier, it was like being in a state of release.

"You are not very adaptable, that is your biggest problem."

How did the bat know that?

"That is the reason why you suffer my friend. Your beliefs are your biggest enemies"
This caught me off guard. I had a very special set of beliefs, which were the pillars of my existence, and now the bat tells me that they are my enemies!!

"How can you say that? I am wherever I am today because of what I have believed in."

"The question dear friend is, that are you happy now?"

"Yes! Very much… almost." My voice was a whimper.

"Your psychic patterns show that you are still in captivation, by deeds and acts done in the past and present lives. The burden of which you still carry.."

"Present lives? I thought the present was just one life."

"There is no one life, this life is made up of many lives, in this and in the other universes."

I was really fascinated by the Bat's teachings. How could this creature know so much?
It was really baffling.

"Your life and all that you see in it is just a fraction of all that is there. As we speak there is another you or several yous co-existing in other dimensions."

This was beyond me.

"Please tell me what else it is that you see, after that I would like to ask a question."

"Yes surely" said the bat.

"I see you as a person who is wanting to be liberated from the chains of human bondage.
A person who is essentially a wanderer, not willing to be held down."

The bat suddenly stopped and seemed to go into deep thought.

"What happened?" I didn't want this thing to stop so soon.

"We are souls of the dead and also symbols of rebirth I am trying to see your new life."

"New life? Hey, I'm still not done with this one! What are you talking about?"

"As we speak, you are losing your old patterns and shedding parts of you that are unwanted."

"But I like a lot of what is there with me. Why should I let go?"

"You can't be a new person till you don't."

"I don't want to, the past is all I have."

"Trust me friend, we are here at this moment of time for a reason."

I had no choice but to become silent though I was feeling a bit lighter and freer now.

"You are now in a state of transition. I have understood your past lives and the reasons that make you do the things that you do."

"You seem to be very quick at all this. How can you see all this so clearly, bat?"

"We bats fly in the dark it isn't difficult for us. We see the unseen and our powers are at their peak in the night.»

"What all will I have to let go of? There is so much that I am not able to let go of.."

"My friend, you can't be released till you don't let go. Let go of your fears, which are your biggest enemies. They have been harbored by you not just for years but in all your lives. That is what you have to let go, out of your heart, your mind and out of your soul. Only then you will be a free spirit."

He seemed to get out of his trance like state as he spoke. As he had rightly said, this meeting was for a reason which I was beginning to realize was far beyond my imagination. In a much deeper sense, it was a healing phase that I was experiencing, something that words could not express.

I had several questions for the bat. But a sort of calm had descended on me. I was being pulled out of the urge to find peace. I was in fact at peace. The feeling was wonderful.

The bat came out of the trance, turned towards me and said, "There is something more that you should to know. You will not be released till you forgive and forget."

"Now that's not easy bat, how is that possible?"

"It is. Your mind, intellect and ego will continue interfering with your freedom unless you are aware of them."

My face I guess revealed my confusion…

The Bat continued…

"To be released, you should be aware of all that you say and all that you do, so everything that you said and did without this awareness keeps returning."

As in several past situations with my feathered friends, I was totally confused.

"How do you know so much?" This was one of the regular questions that I had always had for these winged creatures.

"We just know all that is not clouded in anyway whatsoever, by anything that humans like being with. Their own thoughts and beliefs. Most of these cause misery to them."

I took a deep sigh after fully grasping all this. The bat had spent a considerable amount of time giving advice and help. All this was so relieving that I had completely forgotten that I had to reach early next morning to finish some pending work. What was surprising that the night just seemed to go on and on.

"The time has come for me to leave my friend. You may now open your eyes."

"But my eyes are already open, I can see you clearly."

"Humans have a habit of seeing with their eyes but that sight is what you believe you see" The bat was talking in riddles, I thought. "So remember to forgive and forget if you wish to be released"

I took a good look at the bat before he started flapping his wings and said, "We bats can't see in the sun, we can see in the darkness..but we still know."

He flew around a bit in the semi dark room and said, "You have been looking for the baby peacock. It has been found."

I was astonished. Yet another creature knew so much about me. Just like the owl had.

"Now open your eyes"

I did so and found myself in broad daylight. I looked at the watch, It was 10 am. I was late for work.

As I settled down at work, I grabbed the paper along with a coffee. It read on one of the pages. 'Stolen baby peacock found. Returned to the gardens near the Governer's bunglow. Gang caught.'

Right below that was another head line. 'The UN declares 2011-2012 as International Year of the Bat.'

With another sip of the coffee, I thought to myself.

"I will visit the peacock family this Sunday and also the old vulture. I am sure he would be able to tell me a thing or two about the bat."

Chapter 18

Meeting with Mrs. Peacock and the Jolly Old Vulture

I was able to make it to the gardens the next Sunday. Mrs. Peacock came running towards me the moment she saw me.

"Junior's back!" she said with elation.

"Yes, came to know." I grinned back at her, "Where was he?"

"There was a gang that was smuggling peacocks and selling them somewhere else. They are now caught."

"Yes, I came to know." I started thinking of the bat.

"It's a good that junior came back safe and sound. You all must be very happy."

"Yes" said Mrs. Peacock visibly excited.

"He's resting for a while. I have told his dad to watch over him."

I looked at Mrs. Peacock and asked her, "But how was he discovered ? Who gave the tip?"

She came and sat next to me, "There was banyan tree just next the place where junior was kept. On hearing his cries a bat family living in that tree called some more bats and together they started swarming the neighborhood. Some environmentalists and bird lovers tried to figure out this activity and found junior as he refused to be quiet."

This was it. The pieces started falling into place.

The bat had done so much that had no suitable words of appreciation. Both for myself and also for the peacock family.

Meeting him, whether in real life or imagination, was truly a life changing and sobering moment.

My feathered friends had given me so much joy and companionship over the months that I felt like a new person. Their guidance and support had been invaluable and truly comforting.

With the busy and stressful life that I had been going through, their very presence was a breather and a break from all that the weekdays had to offer.

I felt a sense of joy and contentment on remembering all the good moments they had given and a bit sad too, knowing that there would be a very remote chance of meeting them again. But I was quite sure that many more such enriching experiences would continue in the days to come.

"Give my regards to Mr. Peacock and a Hi to junior too!" I said.

I got ready to leave, as the sun started setting. I wanted to retire early for the night for a change as the last few weeks of late nights had taken their toll.

"I will leave now, take care. I will meet up with my Vulture friend on the way back."

"The Vulture?" Mrs. Peacock came close to the fence. She looked at me sadly, "Don't you know?"

"Know what?"

"He passed away last week. His old age got the better of him. He had said, to give you his regards the next time you came here."

I went home, had a quiet dinner and switched off the lights.

Chapter 19

The Dove

The next week began with loads of work. No time to think, eat or even to breathe easy. I was reaching a saturation point, so high that the breaking point appeared within sight.

I slowly started reflecting on a lot of things. The past, the present and the future swam right in front of my eyes. Coupled with thoughts of the Vulture, life was becoming quite a drag. I was getting weary by the second and losing interest in work slowly but surely I was feeling mentally and emotionally drained and was just short of being a wreck.

As they say "It happens".

I had been able to pull through so far due to my feathered friends, but now it seemed as if all was literally in the dumps.

I was in half a mind to take a long vacation and go off to some faraway place. Work was not permitting this and we were in the middle of a not-so-great business cycle, so more time had to be spent with the team. Strategizing, and executing new ideas, countering competition was all that a day's work boiled down to.

I picked up a few music CDs the next Sunday, started the car and drove out of the city. After almost an hour I reached a vantage point in a slightly hilly terrain. I stopped the car and walked out, stretched my legs, and strolled down a path, till a beautiful scenic spot caught my eye. One could see for miles in the valley ahead with greenery all around. I sat on a rock and took a deep breath.

After what seemed an eternity, staring into nowhere and letting the cool breeze play its music in my ears, I came to the conclusion that this so called happiness was quite a subjective thing.

We did things because they were meant to give happiness.

I was always of the opinion that it made no sense in doing something that everyone did.

"Why?" I'd ask myself. "Just because something makes someone happy, is it necessary it should give happiness to me as well?"

And here I was sitting all alone, trying to convince myself that all was good, everything was fine because I was doing the right things that lead to happiness.

Happiness... hah! Searching for it is all a waste of time.

I opened a bottle of water and had a few thirsty gulps, spilled some of it on the rock too.

"Oh what the .." . I emptied the bottle on the rock in exasperation.

It was the outset of evening around 5 pm, as the sun was preparing to set.

Time to go back to the jungle with the wild animals... or is it the city? Ha!

As I got up to leave, with a heavy heart and still no answers to my questions, I heard a sound behind.

It was a sort of a "Oo-wah-hooo, hoo-hoo".

I turned around and saw a beautiful white bird sitting next to the water that I had spilled on the rock.

"You shouldn't waste water my friend" the bird said, "It's precious!"

Though the light in the sky was steadily dimming and I had to squint to see properly, the bird stood out and was very much visible in the fading light. She started drinking the water thirstily.

She was a dove.

She looked like a goddess or an angel that had descended from the heavens. Her very sight brought a strange kind of calm and peace within, something that was just to be experienced. I was least expecting this to happen, however considered it to be some sort of good luck.

"Luck?" I thought to myself.

Yes perhaps, as the dove's appearance, out of nowhere, must have had a reason.

As I looked at this winged marvel of nature, she continued to drink from the little concave hollows in the rock, where the water had settled.

Not knowing how to respond, I continued looking at the dove. The feeling was quite 'heavenly'. After a few seconds, the dove said a polite "Thank you" and looked at me.

"How did you come to be here?" I queried.

"Oh I was flying by, felt thirsty and saw you emptying the water bottle so came down from the sky."

I couldn't help but stare at the dove. She was so pure and divine against the dark backdrop of the night sky that I calmed down further.

"You don't seem to be with your friends... you came to this forest alone?" I asked, being the inquisitive kind as I was.

"Actually, I was in a cage with the other doves being put up for sale. I escaped."

"Oh I see, yes freedom... we all crave for it. Why didn't the other doves join you?"

"They have forgotten who they are. They get food and a cozy cage, even when left to fly they return to their cage in the evening."

"How is that possible? Birds are meant to fly in the skies."

"That is for humans to understand." The dove started drinking again. She was still thirsty and looked tired too.

"So where are you headed now?"

"Where ever my heart desires. I have yet to see and learn a lot. It wasn't possible back there."

Wanting to go home, I decided to leave. Besides, the dove may have wanted to rest for a while.

"I guess it's time for me to head back to the city, you must have come from there I guess. How much is it forty miles?"

"Forty? Oh no" the dove said, "Let's see... I have done about 5000 miles till now."

I decided that this revelation merited for me to stay back and spend some more time with the dove. I sat down next to her on the same rock.

"Don't you think you're being a bit impractical?"

"About what?" The dove asked.

"Look you escaped from the cage and flew away. But 5000 miles… and you still don't know where you're going."

"So, what difference does it make? At least I'm free now!"

"Look," I tried explaining to her, "It's a wild world out there, and you're all alone, doesn't that bother you?"

She sat down on the rock and made herself more comfortable.

"I have thought along those lines also. But you would agree, I can't just go back, can I?"

"No, I'm not telling you to do so. All I'm asking you is how long are you just going to continue flying like this, that too without knowing where you're going?"

She thought for a moment. Night was fast approaching and the dimly lit stars were just about beginning to show in the skies. I was not sure what time I'd be reaching home, however I hoped to come to some conclusion with the dove on this conversation.

The dove was very innocent as she had chosen to fly for so long on her own. She was completely unaware where she was headed. At the same time, I thought that she was quite brave to just move out and explore on her own.

After what seemed like a few minutes of silence and deep thought, the dove said, "It's true that my family and friends back there must be having quite a comfortable life, with all the good food in the world, water and someone to care for them."

She again fell silent. I had faced several similar situations in life, whether to stay in the comfort zone or to just move out of it, I felt in the heart of my hearts the joy which the dove must have experienced by getting away from the cage, but the fact remained that she was all on her own with no companions and still no clear direction in which to go.

I started wondering whether the dove was on the right or wrong track.

The dove was pondering over the situation. I was expecting her to conclude by agreeing with whatever I told her. After all, practically speaking, it was the safest and right thing for her to just settle down rather than continue flying into the wilderness.

Finally she broke her silence and looked pleased, "You know something friend? What you just said does make sense. I have given it some thought."

"So?" I was glad to see that the dove had agreed with what I had told her.

She took one more helping of water from the rock crevice and said, "I think you're wrong."

I was taken aback by this answer.

The dove continued to drink the water.

"How do you say that?" I wanted an answer without further delay.

"Because, to choose comfort is one's choice. I chose not to have it."

"What's wrong in being comfortable? We long for it."

"Yes it's nice to be comfortable, but after a while I realized that I was getting complacent."

"Oh so one day you just decide to take off and fly 5000 miles?"

"So?" If the dove had eyebrows, She would surely have raised one.

"So, there's nothing wrong with it dove friend? Just where are you headed and what is your destination?"

"I have chosen to fly, I'm doing just that. What's wrong with that ?"

"But you know where you're headed."

"Is it important?" the dove asked. "Look, you humans get caught up in so much of reasoning that you forget the fun of life. You forget to live for the moment and in all this you lose yourselves. What's wrong if I'm just flying. I'm getting to see new places, new things. I have learnt so much more in all these days."

Sure. That too was a point of view.

"Don't you think the company of your fellow doves would give you more happiness?"

"It would," said the dove. "I do think of them often. But is it necessary to do what the others are doing?"

That was exactly what I had asked myself on the rock just before the dove had arrived. What a coincidence !!!

"No dear dove. But all alone, it's not exactly a safe place up there and also some humans are fond of hunting down animals and birds, if you know what I mean. The sky is also full of so many other birds that look for prey."

"Does that mean that I should stop flying?"

The dove's replies were just a barrage of counter questions.

"No dove, I am not saying that. But it would have made more sense if you had more doves with you."

"I tried convincing the other doves to move out. None of them agreed. In fact I met many on the way. They all had their own agenda."

116

"Hmm... that seems to be a valid reason." The dove had answered all that I had to ask very reasonably.

"A last question for you. Give me one good reason why you think you are better off now than the friends and family you left behind."

The dove flapped her wings flew up a little and came back to the rock. She said with utmost happiness.

"My wings are stronger."

I concluded two things. Firstly that that she kept on flying without even knowing of the perils in the sky, and secondly, that she was brave. Even after realizing what could happen, she still stuck to her path. She looked at the sky and was enjoying the breeze that was blowing across the mountains.

It came to my mind that my life was not very different from the dove's. The only difference was that she had wings.

To think of it, this itself made all the difference. The dove had wings. Fascinated as I was with these creatures, I had developed over the years a sense of awe and respect for them. Not only because of their ability to fly but also to freely move around unlike us human beings.

Apart from that, these birds were historic, prehistoric and even mythological. It was hard to believe that their very existence was as old as the human race, perhaps even older.

The dove was right because her wings were stronger, and over the journey she was surer of her abilities to fly and survive.

"It's a bit late now, may I leave?" I finally asked the dove

She replied "The time is yours, you can do whatever you wish to do with it."

"Yes you're right, we can choose to do whatever with it. Circumstances can change though."

The Dove thought for a moment.

"Yes circumstances can change, but what we do in those circumstances is equally important."

She had a point there.

"True. However all circumstances are not in our control."

"You're right. If they were, then life would become very predictable because we would be able to get whatever we wanted."

There was a heavy silence for some time.

I got up to leave. It was not an easy decision. The dove continued to enjoy her blissful state seemingly unaware that I had gotten up.

"What are you thinking?' I asked.

"Oh nothing really, I was just remembering my family and friends. We did have some good time together though we were caged most of the time. My mom used to tell me stories."

"Well… OK Dove, I have to say goodbye now as I have to head home."

I started leaving when the dove flew and sat on my arm. "Well there is one more good reason why I'm better off than my friends and family whom I left behind in the cage."

"What's that?"

"I got the chance to meet you."

It was a long and silent journey back home.

Chapter 20

The Rooster and Hen Affair

I had the opportunity of going out of town, to a village for a few days. We had a wonderful evening with a bonfire, games, songs and food on the first night and retired quite late to our individual cottages. Some slept on the cots outside.

No sooner had I slipped into deep sleep, with dreams of various kinds, than I was unceremoniously woken up by a sound. Considering the time, it was not one of the most pleasant sounds, and was coming right from right next to where my drowsy head lay on the cot.

The rooster seemed to be enjoying his morning call as the sun was slowly rising from behind the trees.

I pleaded, "Could you stop that please?"

The Rooster wasn't amused at being asked to be silent. He crowed, "That will not be possible sir."

"And why so ? People here are trying to sleep." I pointed to the cottages all around.

"Sleep is meant for the night sir. Dawn has already arrived".

I did not want to argue with the rooster, after all a Rooster would not understand the way we lived. The rooster continued his 'wake up' call and after he seemed satisfied, he walked up to me.

"I can't blame you for the way you humans live. We Roosters need to follow our own system."

Now that was one topic that I was ready to debate on at any point of time. I had done it quite often with dad who always stressed on punctuality, discipline and a systematic approach to life. I had many a times felt the importance of these but this 'exactness' of living was not much to my fancy. I was ready to take on the rooster on this subject.

"You are right Rooster, the way you live your life may not be liked by many of us. I am surely one of them"

The Rooster turned in another direction and became quiet for a while. A rather well fed hen strolled into the area pecking at whatever she seemed to find edible. The Rooster did not take his eyes off the hen for even a second. It was an eye of concern.

"This way of life gives meaning to what we do you see," the Rooster said, looking at me for a second. "By following our daily routine, we are able to use our time better."

He continued looking at the hen till she came near us. He then said "Meet my wife!" The hen walked closer and stood next him.

"Speaking of system, I would not have got my wife without it."

"How is that? How did you two meet?" There was still plenty of time for the others to wake up and I was fully awake.

"It's a long story. I will have to tell it in parts."

"Ok…" I was all ears.

"We had an affair and eloped."

The hen came closer and sat next to the rooster with an approving 'Cluck' and looked at both of us.

"I was one of 5 chicks born to our mom on a farm not far from here. I had a happy childhood playing with the others. The nights were spent around the barn, chatting with the cows, horses and occasional pigs that ran around the place. Our owner was a nice person who took good care of us. Then one day a neighboring farmer came to meet our owner."

The hen clucked in acknowledgement.

"He had to go to his wife's village, far away for a few days so he got his hens and roosters in a carriage to be left with us as there was no one to take care of them. One of the infants in that lot was this lady here!!" He looked at the hen and gave a gentle smile.

"It took a day or two for us to get friendly with the other hens and roosters as they were of a slightly different breed. However our habits were more or less the same. We started playing together after two days. She was a bit different as she did not mingle with the others, which had caught my attention from day one."

"Ah, so you were eyeing her from the first day, is it?" Couldn't help asking.

"Well it was nothing of that sort you see, it's just that I was more of the playful type and she seemed just the opposite. That's all."

"But what was the reason for that?" I picked up a blade of grass from the ground and started fiddling with it.

Sunil Bhatia

"That's exactly the question that was in my mind," said the rooster. Though we were not more than a few months old, a few things could be understood. So I went up to her."

I was sure to hear an interesting tale, as always my feathered friends never ceased to offer one.

"She was sitting at the edge of the farm, all alone looking at the setting sun one evening lost in her own thoughts. I was a bit hesitant to go nearer as we still knew nothing about each other."

I was almost at the edge of the boulder on which I was sitting. Thankfully no one was still awake. It had been a long night of partying for most and everyone was catching up on sleep. I had backed out of the celebrations earlier and gone for a stroll, so felt rested despite having been woken up by the Rooster call.
The hen started clucking again as if she remembered something. The rooster started telling his story which almost took me back to the moment that he was so fondly recalling.

"It's been almost 20 years since that day you know" The rooster Said, as he lovingly looked at her. "I can still recall each and every moment of that day. She didn't notice at first that I was standing next to her for a while, till I asked her why she was sitting there all alone."

"She said she liked being alone and it was nice to be in peace and quiet. She had been like that since the beginning."

"She did seem quite at ease as she spoke. There was a strange kind of calm around her." The rooster paused and looked as if he was back in that moment. I interrupted his day dream as I was curious to know what happened next, "So what did you say?" I asked.

"I asked her why she didn't feel like enjoying with the others. They all looked happy, having fun while she was just sitting there all alone."

"She very wisely said to me that happiness was one thing, contentment another."

The Rooster continued, "Then I asked her what was wrong if the other chicks are happy? She just smiled and said to me, "I like it this way, they like it that way, is there anything wrong in that?""

The hen had a point too.

"I was curious to know that why she wasn't like the others at her young age she wasn't behaving like her siblings and she had responded to this question simply by saying that age is all in the mind, I feel no reason to be like the others."

The hen seemed to have a way of her own, and the best thing was that she seemed fine with it and the way she was living her life.

"In fact, I'm quite comfortable the way I am." She said.

"Comfortable" sounded like a nice word and for the first time it was making sense in what the hen was saying.

The hen and rooster looked at each other for a while then looked at me. I was deeply engrossed in the rooster's tale as they sat in front of me.

"She seemed to be right, I thought at that moment of time." said the rooster, "We spend so much time in running around that we do not even have time to be with ourselves for a moment, and she was with herself all the time."

The hen was still quiet and looked so relaxed there that it dawned on me that a lot could be learnt from her.

The rooster went on, "She has been very good at judging situations, and has always given the best advice whenever it was required"

"What happened after that?" I asked both of them.

"We sat there till the sun went down, and continued talking for a very long time in the dark, way into the night. Our conversation just seemed to go on and on. It's strange how just talking with someone could be so enjoyable and relieving at the same time."

It was around 7 am at that time and there was still no sign of anyone waking up in the camp. "Your wakeup call never woke up anyone Mr. Rooster." I said with a smile.

"Not everyone can appreciate the beauty of the rising sun, only we roosters have that good fortune. Besides, time is ticking, it waits for no one. We know more about it than anyone else."

"Can you go and take a look at the kids? They must have woken up." The hen spoke for the first time. Her voice was soft and bright at the same time.

"Yes my dear, I'll be back in a moment." The rooster went off in a hurry.

As we were left alone, the hen turned to me "We have five young ones you see, they normally wake up around this time."

"That's good ma'am. If you don't mind my asking, what did you see in the rooster that made you decide to be with him?" After asking this question I felt I may have asked it too soon. I had only just met the Rooster and the Hen after all.

"Oh that's alright. You see we do have certain similar qualities but by and large, he is quite the opposite. He likes talking a lot unlike me."

"Looking at you two together, I'm sure there must be something more to it ma'am. Am I right?" I urged her on.

"Oh yes. He's very good at predicting the future. Almost everything that he says comes true. Roosters, you see, are part of the cosmic forces of nature so they know which way things are going to move. They are rightfully called the timekeepers. They can also tell which way the wind is blowing."

The rooster came back. "I gave them something to eat my dear. They were asking for you." The hen got up and shook her feathers out a bit. "Its my turn to go now. You two have a good time!" She waddled away towards her coop. Now it was the rooster and me left alone.

"Your wife was saying that you're good at predictions."

"Oh it's nothing really" The rooster said quite modestly.

"No no dear rooster, it really is a rare talent to look into the future and see what's going to happen. How do you do it?". The 'dear' came out of nowhere.

I was certainly not going to lose anytime in getting some questions answered. The sun was steadily rising and the whole camp would be waking. The rooster perched on the rock next to me and gazed into the distance. He softly started talking, "So as we were speaking before I left, you see time is ticking and you want to know a few things because you've realized its importance now."

He was right.

"Can you really tell the future? I have a few questions to ask."
He looked at the sun, took a deep breath and gave another one of his calls. He was lost in the magnificence of the warmth that the day was beginning to bring. He sat down looking at the heavenly object in the east and asked, "Ok. What do you want to know?"

"Firstly, how do you look into the future?"

He continued looking at the sun and said calmly, "You see my friend what you call the future is actually a probability."

I looked at the rooster with a puzzled face, which the rooster probably saw, "Let me clarify, we roosters are good at knowing the possible outcomes. The most probable one in the future. Since we understand human nature well, it is not difficult for us to know what will happen to an individual or even in circumstances which involve many. In many cases you would be amazed to know that several of us are living similar lives. Since we are separated by miles, we don't come to know of it."

The rooster continued looking at the sun lovingly and with a tinge of nostalgia, he spoke again.

"I felt the same way when I had met my wife 20 years ago, I could see a possible future with her."

"Possible means that you were not sure of it, right Mr. Rooster?"

"No, possible means the one scenario that stands out as feasible compared to others that don't seem so great."

"Ok, could you tell me what's there in the sun that you follow it so diligently?"

"The sun, my friend, for centuries has awed all. Some say that life came from the sun itself. There is a cycle for everything. When we predict the future we know which part of the cycle to look at."

"All that is fine Mr. Rooster, but certain things, infact many things that are unprecedented and unexpected. How do you explain those?"

"These incidents are also part of the cycle my friend. We think that they are unexpected without knowing that one event leads to another and so on and so forth."

"I fail to understand how, many of us live similar lives, as you said a while ago."

"If you see, everyone has moments of happiness, sorrow, peace, bonding, elation and a range of emotions. They may be in varying proportions and intensities. To begin with, this is the first stage at which our lives are similar"

"Hmm… Interesting, I never looked at life from this perspective."

I was hoping that no one would wake up soon. I looked at the tents, straining my ears to hear a sound. As luck would have it, no one had woken up yet. After a brief period of silence I asked the rooster, "So what are the other stages where our lives are similar?"

The rooster got up.

"Ah, these are even more interesting. But I need to leave for the moment as my family is waiting for me. We can perhaps speak tomorrow morning around 5 am."

"That early?" I was on a holiday so had no intention of waking up at that time.

"I will wake you up my friend."

After another night of celebrations around the bonfire, I dropped onto the cot at 4.30 am. Soon I was in a deep slumber when the wake-up call of the Rooster got in the way of bliss.

I opened one eye and saw Mr. Rooster looking at me, "Wakey wakey my friend, its 5 am!"

I was really sleepy and couldn't even open my eyes when I slurred at him, "Tell you what Mr. Rooster, I would really like to sleep a little more."

"Ok, then I'm gone, I believe you're all leaving after a few hours."

"Wait! I'll try getting up." I scrambled out of the cot, rubbing my eyes. I splashed water on my face and in that groggy state said, "Go on... I'm listening."

He came and sat next to me. I could see him looking bright and fresh, silhouetted against the bonfire ambers. The early morning rays of light followed.

"Ah yes! Coming back to our point of discussion, you see our lives are quite similar in many ways. The proportions and timings however may vary from one entity to another."

"Ok, point taken Mr. Rooster, however all our lives can't be exactly can they? You're such an early riser, something that I'm miles away from."

"It is necessary my friend, to drive evil spirits away."

"E..e..evil spirits ? What do you mean?" Now there was this fascinating little twist in the tale.

"Yes, we Roosters herald the coming of the dawn and our morning call is a message to these evil spirits to get moving. We tell all living beings to wake up and start a new day."

"What or who are these spirits and what do they want? Do they only come out in the night?"

I hope I had not asked too many questions all at once.

"There are good spirits also my friend. They are around all the time, just a little more active in the night because all the living creatures are sleeping."

"And what do you mean by active?"

"It means that they try to find a medium to enter into the physical world again. There are the spirits that do so to finish unfinished business. Sometimes it's a good spirit that just wants to pass on a message to someone."

As the Rooster spoke, he gained my respect. He was free to share his invaluable knowledge with humans and the more he spoke, the less it seemed that I had knowledge of life.

"I have also sensed this at times, Mr. Rooster, the presence of someone or something around. I have not been able to put a finger on it. Perhaps these are the spirits that you speak of."

"There are many around even as we speak my friend. They hear and see us all the time."

"Do you mean to say that you can also see them Mr. Rooster? How do you know that they are near?"

The Rooster came closer and said in a whisper, "While you were sleeping, one of the spirits got inside you."

I was shocked but not truly believed in what I was hearing, "This is a little hard to believe rooster friend. How is it possible that another soul is inside me, especially when I'm as normal as before."

"That is how it appears to be my friend, as we speak, this soul is quietly hiding inside you and will come out when it feels right to do so."

"Why don't you drive it away?"

"Because it's a good soul. We only chase away the evil ones. Be at ease, it will go away with the passing sun as it is also chasing light to see the physical world which it has left behind."

"All this is quite fascinating rooster, is this true even for the evil spirits?"

"No they are the dark spirits and negate light with their dark energy."

"Aah..so its good vs evil isn't it?"

"The rooster took a little stroll and said "Yes you could say so. It's all within us, good, bad, we just need to look inside."

The rooster started his call again as I pondered over these words. It was almost time to get ready and leave. The Hen and Rooster had given me good company and it was indeed interesting to know so much about the way things worked in their realm of life.

"Why does evil seem to win most of the time and good have to suffer so much?" I probed before time ran out.
"The good and evil that you speak of are all within us. We choose to follow whichever suits us depending on our mental and emotional state in our journey of life."

"That does not answer the question dear Rooster."

"Evil, or the dark energies are just the opposite of good or light. We keep moving from one state to another. Yes, we are attracted more towards darkness as we are essentially beings with light in its purest form. To answer your question, Evil never really wins, it's just the people stop being and doing good."

I had never thought on these lines.

"Needless to say, the dark days that one sees, only help us in appreciating the depth of life, live in all its dimensions, physical and metaphysical."

"Hey we're getting late!" My friends were calling out as they were ready to leave.

I got up, feeling a bit sad to leave the company of yet another feathered friend.

"How will I know when to go the right way?"

The rooster gave another call and said "Look inside, you will see the light."

As we left, the sun rose into the sky spreading its warmth in all its brilliance. With images of the rooster in my mind, I fell asleep in the car as we travelled homeward.

Chapter 21

The Humming Bird and Her Message

I was on leave, partly on vacation, out of the country, and with generally nothing to do. The much needed vacation was about to come to an end and I decided to spend some time in a park that I had noticed a few days ago while travelling.

It had some of the most beautiful flowers and the place in itself was quite alive with families and their pets, children and even the elderly, would visit to sit around, chat and even to take a break. I went there with the same intention of idling around and dozing off on the grass.

It was a wonderful day and I was doing just that, when a faint buzzing sound came close to my ears. It went on increasing, then decreasing. It sounded more like a steady hum. I opened my eyes to see a tiny bird that was doing the rounds from flower to flower. I was lying down between two flower beds, the little winged creature kept crossing my ears. She seemed quite engrossed in her activity and I started watching her with interest. I had heard about these birds but only got the opportunity to see a humming bird for the first time, which is the smallest bird, they say.

She was quite unique as she could fly forwards, backwards, up and down with ease and precision, all the while connecting with the tubular flowers which were neatly arranged all around. She eventually noticed me looking at her.

"What a wonderful bird you are!" I exclaimed. "It's been so mesmerizing just watching you go around the flowers the way you do."
The birdie came nearer and said teeny "Thanks," all the while still hovering around in the air.

I realized that she was probably this way, to keep on flying.

"Don't you get tired of flying around all the time?"

The birdie came nearer and said, "No it's actually a pleasure to be around this place, can't waste even a second."

She went off to some other flowers and came back.

"Besides, the nectar gives us all the energy we need to keep going, so it's ok."
I was wondering what to say when she came back again and said, "What are you doing before and after the summers next year?"

"Nothing planned so far birdie, is there anything interesting happening?"

"Yes, the annual bird convention is happening in the Philippines, there's a huge bird sanctuary there. You might like attending it."

All this sounded so good that I jumped up from my reclining position and looked at her with an eager face. I exclaimed, "That would be a great experience, what would they be discussing there?"

"There would be all sorts of Migratory birds, around 40,000 of them, who would be voicing their concerns on the future of their species on our planet, even those on the brink of extinction."

"I'm look forward to it. What about you hummingbird?"

"I can reach there as its around 3000 miles from here, Its just that I'm about to start my family life soon and would be flying towards the western hemisphere to settle down there. You could mention my name once you reach there though."

"Thank you so much my friend for the information." I said to the humming bird, but I thought to myself, "3000 miles… Wow!"

"Please pass on my message of joy, happiness and love to all the fellow birds attending and tell them that there is still hope for us if we communicate our language to the human beings," said the little bird to me.

We were there together till the park became empty. She was gracious enough to sing one of her songs by sunset. She was a ruby throated hummingbird.

I went home after watching a movie at a nearby theatre, all the while thinking of the humming bird and her message. I looked up the bird sanctuary over the internet as told by the birdie. I found the Philippines Tourism site and on further searching, found the Island of Olango. It seemed that many more feathered friends were about to cross my path and touch my life in the months ahead.

(End of Part 1)

The Book of Poems
Part 1

Surreal/Mystical Poems

1) The Magical Box-Part 1

Felt like letting go
Of all my hopes, dreams
And aspirations
It seemed so.

Meaning had left
All sensibility behind
Nothing seemed to remind
Me of my self

Time was on the go.

Sunil Bhatia

Then there appeared
In my dreams

An object of strange desire
That imagination had perhaps conspired.

Like life sometimes plays
A hoax, as we see
Even day has its ghosts
Though we may not agree.

There it was
In front of my eyes
I looked at it like a fox
It was not made up of lies

It was

A magical box.

2) The Magical Box-Part 2

There were days
And months and years
That had brought with them
Many cheers

Yet time was such
That I wanted it to flow
Happiness was moving
There was still much left to tow.

The magical box
Was made to be quite a show
Went near it
As curiosity began to grow.

Not knowing what to expect,
Opened it, real slow
When,
There was a pleasant sound.

Like music to the ears
Driving out all my fears
Soft words filled the room
And floated around.

"What is it that your
Heart desires?
What all do you
Want to know?"

Then,

The magical box began to glow.

3) The Magical Box-Part 3

Then, there was
A bright white light
Which changed to
Colors of a rainbow.

The box seemed
To summon me
To go near it
Thoughts came so.

Awed a bit
By these sights
With desires surging like
A new candle lit.

Burning the wick
I could not believe it
When clouds appeared
Then scattered...

A beautiful blue hand rose
Out of the golden mist
Its finger moved down
Line by line, by the wrist.

The sound came once again
"This is your wish list
All is fine
But one thing you have missed."

What could it be?
That had not
Crossed my mind.
There was surely something

That I had to find.
I had dreams to be fulfilled
But a few
There was surely something

That
The magical box knew.

4) The Magical Box-Part 4

"Yes I do"
The voice thus spoke
"There's always a part of you
That's still unexplored.

So, it's likely
That you don't know.
For its something that
Has not been seen."

"What do you mean?
I do know who I am!"
The voice replied
"But you may not remember

Where you have been."

The blue hand dived
Into the magical box
And came out with
A peacock feather pen.

Started studying the
Invisible lines again.
It set me thinking
The mist turned purple then.

"I Have run through my wishes
Have known what I want
Have seen all that's needed
Tell me will they come?"

"You have put your wishes
Which are very fair,
But what you've forgotten
Is what you will share."

"You've said what you wanted
Except if you care
To give something in return
It's not mentioned anywhere."

The hand stopped this time,
A scent filled the air
I had nothing much to do
But stand there and stare.

"That is going to be
Your most crucial wish
Tell me for its time now
For me to vanish."

The magical box then began getting
Smaller and smaller and smaller.

5) The Contract

Still remember the day
When I was summoned
Before landing on mother earth
Made out of water, air, fire and clay.

Was standing after a while
In a room before the Father,
The Son, and the Holy ghost,
Was not sure to be grim, or to smile.

There was cool air
Around the place
As scented spirits flittered
Surrounding the staircase.

"Congratulations my boy!
You're day has come
You've made it this time
You are the chosen one."

Looked on to the table
Wanting sense to enable
A reason for this prospect
For them, everyone did respect.

"But I'm happy here father
To stay with you, is what I'd do rather
You're sending me to earth
Is this what the waiting was worth?"

"Questions you may have many
And answers there are few
Finding the meaning of life
Is what should be your view"

"OK, as you say father
Tell me now what to do
I'd like to see if what lies there
Has more than what I knew."

"Then it is done, you may depart
Before you leave, you have to start
Reading this, what we have for you
It tells what's needed to be true."

"What is this father?"
I exclaimed,
"Have never known this,
Please explain."

"This, my son is
The Contract,
The act,
The fact."

The contract ran into several pages,
Hundreds of clauses,
Things to do
And many not to.

"This is an understanding
That you will follow,
The codes of conduct
As said in the contract"

Before I could react
Was given to sign it, a pen
And led to a chamber
To read it again.

Many years have passed
Since then,
Had almost forgotten
The contract, when

Sunil Bhatia

Remember having read it
It is strange, for it
Was the sole purpose for which all till now
Has arranged.

Am still trying to put together
The words page by page,
For following them, stage by stage
Was to decide my mortal age.

Still have a memory of the way
In which had even prayed
To have a life, and to be
Content as it stayed

The contract still remains
To be honored
Over many tomorrows,
If they are there again

Many yesterdays are left
Wanting to keep
The contract alive
With all that it was instilled.

And it was the last page
Written in bold,
And as was told
Which said that the doors

To the Father, the Son
And the Holy Ghost
Will open once again
Only after the contract

Is fulfilled.

Love Poems

1) There must be a reason

There must be a reason
Why we met,
Why two strangers
Were caught in a net

Out of nowhere
This meaningful, unexplainable
Sympathy arose,
And made us transpose

To a world
We can never forget,
There must be a reason
Why we met.

Why the dawn happened,
Why the night came,
Why it almost
Drove us insane,

To situations
Never dreamt of,
To conversations
Which we still don't regret.

Such were the moments
Not easy to correct,
Or resurrect,
However much we inspect

Sunil Bhatia

Into the hallows of time
Where all our pasts,
Present and futures
Are set.

There must be a reason
Why we met,
There must have been something
We were trying to get.

2) Turn the Tables

Turn the Tables,
Turn the time,
Turn it anywhere,
Anytime

Look around,
Look in my eyes
You'll see the stranger
Who had died

A thousand years,
Ten thousand times
Its all the same
But still its fine!

We are the creatures
Of this faith
That binds us here
In endless space

I have known you
You have known me
We've known each other
Since eternity

I have known you
You have known me
We know it all
Still we can't see

I have known you,
You have known me
Yes it was love
But now we're free

Sunil Bhatia

I have known you
You have known me
The pain reaches
Infinity.

I have known you
You have known me
Still we accept
Our destinies

Turn the tables
Turn the time
Turn it anywhere
Anytime.

3) I once knew you

I once knew you,
It was a long time
From now,

I once knew you,
And we drifted apart
Somehow.

I once knew you,
When it was too good
To be true,

And I once knew you,
Now there is very little
That we can do.

I once knew you,
All is forgotten
Once we bade adieu,

And I once knew you,
As someone with a different
Point of view.

I once knew you
As a friend,
To trust unto
The end.

And I once knew you
As one to whom happiness was
Still, yet never due.

I once knew you.
As the only person
I ever only knew.

Sunil Bhatia

And I once knew you
As the first drop.
Of early morning dew.

I once knew you
As the ocean
Befriending storms

And I once knew you
As the one with ever
Open arms.

I once knew you
Yes, I once knew you
And I know that

You knew me too...

4) *Maybe*

Maybe you're right
Maybe I'm wrong
Maybe there's nothing
Left for long

Maybe it's time
That I moved on
Maybe its fine
If I was gone

Maybe we live
To make our dreams
Maybe we feel
That's all it seems

Maybe you listen
To what I say
Maybe you know
For what I stay

Maybe there's something
That I like
Maybe I'll get it
Day and night

Maybe I'm sure
That you'll say don't
Maybe you will
Maybe you won't

Maybe there's someone
On your mind
Maybe it's me
Somewhere behind

Sunil Bhatia

Maybe that's why
Today's the same
Maybe tomorrow
Will change again

Maybe you're right
Maybe I'm wrong
Maybe we'll just
Carry along..

5) Karmic Connection

It was a meeting
Sometime ago,
We met in an instance,
Meant to come and go.

We went our own ways,
Was destiny's choice
And all was forgotten
Until on this day.

There was a strange feeling
That can't be explained
The moment of truth
Was meant to be regained.

A karmic connection
Making people meet,
It was something magical,
Something unexplained.

No distance of any kind
Can keep us apart,
The Karmic connection
Will show us the art.

Fantasy-Story Poems

1) Tunnel of eternity

It was very late after the grind,
Was sleeping in delirium to unwind,
When there was a bright colorful light,
Flashing in places in parts of my mind.

Saw a circular motion,
In the line of sight,
Connecting to another place,
Centuries ago, to another life,

That was lived so.

The tunnel of eternity had
A strange magnetic pull,
Drawing me endlessly
Ferrying my hull.

Showing what had happened
Flowing in this journey,
Making things clearer,
So simple, yet so holy.

I stayed asleep for it so wondrously appealed,
The tunnel of eternity was infinitely
Connected to where I had now entwined,
And then it showed another path,

Like the lines on a hand
How new time was planned.
The tunnel of eternity
Was the moment of truth,

And freedom from the damned.

2) Lunar Fantasy

The sun shone its rays
Into the eyes of its children.
Breathing life on the other side
As they saw the world around.

Heaven and earth
Disappeared,
And all became one
Between the sky, water and ground.

All could be seen through
Opaque walls of human ingenuity,
The nothingness around was all
Because of the lunar fantasy.

Everything became part of the flow,
Feelings became the answer to
The show.
As the moonlight began to grow.

No reasons, no questions to the effect,
The cause itself became
The motion for one to know.

There is hardly anything that
Cannot be explained,

All makes sense as
The Lunar fantasy removes
The pretense,
Sowing seeds as the consequence.

All is one, one is all.
Something now begins to call.
As the light now shows the way,
Still far from the call of day.

Sunil Bhatia

Illusions large or small,
Will follow the shadows all
Let the Lunar fantasy shine
As it lights up the hall.

3) Twisted path of fate

Who said it was straight,
Makes one contemplate,
Leading one to certainty,
Golden spoon and plate.

The eye of the monster,
The tail of the prey,
A story first rate,
Twisted path of fate.

The angels in heaven,
The corridors to hell,
The graveyard inscription,
Is all left to tell.

The future of happiness,
Freedom from the past,
Life's one only mate,
Twisted path of fate.

Reasons all declined,
Emotions confined,
Erupting volcanoes,
Defining their time,

Oceans of serenity,
Vacation sublime,
And then finally,
A breathtaking light.

With pipers playing sweet music
Waiting at the gates,
A welcome to eternity,
Not early or late.

After all the heart burns,
Perhaps, there's more wait,
Another one of those wretched turns,
Of the twisted path of fate.

4) Compass of destiny

So here I am again,
Caught between the future, past
And the present domain.

Time a companion at every moment,
Ready to leave me behind
At the drop of a hat,

Its vital component.

Put my fingers in my pocket,
And take out
The compass of destiny.

Its needle is swinging
In wild ecstasy,
Directions are a joke

As the compass is still
Trying to find reason
In its search of temporary sanity.

The wind is blowing,
Directionless at every moment,
As the compass of destiny

Reconciles its triumph
In the complacency
Of the devil's advocacy.

After a while,
The needle becomes still
Like a hermit on a hill.

The compass of destiny
Is all that's left
In the turbulence of life's storm.

Blowing freely at its will.

5) Castle of mirrors

The castle of mirrors
Stood atop a hill.
It was someplace different,
Where dreams were fulfilled.

The wild waves were lashing
On rocks all around,
The castle of mirrors
Did in secrets abound.

One day a boatman
Happened to lose way,
He stumbled onto something
On what none could say.

The castle of mirrors
Had souls all around,
Trying to keep everything
That they once had found.

His lost lonely spirit
Reflected in time,
The castle of mirrors,
Showed him his own mind.

He had to return
To where he belonged,
The castle of mirrors
Gave all that he longed.

It may still exist
Somewhere in the gale,
The castle of mirrors
Is now just a tale.

Self Poems

1) Cocoon

It's been a while now, can tell
Being here with my thoughts,
Have not heard the sights, sounds and smells
Locked up in solitary confinement, in this cell.

The cocoon is all around me,
Spun with its silky spell,
The cocoon is where I'm bound now,
This is where I dwell.

Hidden from the evil world,
Far away from hell,
The cocoon is where I hide now,
Far from the tolling bell.

It's been quite a waiting,
Since those caterpillar ways,
When life was slow and steady,
Such were the good old days.

One day I'll be a butterfly,
Flying far away,
Till then I'll just be happy,
Tucked warmly today.

There is no haste to move out,
This heaven is sheer bliss,
There is so much of happiness,
Something that can't be missed.

The cocoon is where dreams are made,
And then left there to rest,
Let me be here for a while more,
Lay cradled in the nest.

162

2) Zombie

Wake up in the morning,
Wash my weary face,
Look into the mirror,
Oh what a disgrace!

Shines the sun so brightly,
Calls out to life again,
Step into the daylight,
Can't sense any pain.

Turned into a zombie,
Living life insane,
There is nothing one can see,
With a scattered brain.

Trying still to focus,
On the only game,
It will set me free one day,
Oh it's such a shame!

Turned into a zombie,
Eyeballs sticking out,
Sleep is now a stranger,
Wish that I could shout.

Turned into a zombie,
Like so many more,
Plodding on the road to hell,
Lets see what's in store.

Turned into a zombie,
Insulated from crime,
A face with no expressions,
What a pantomime!

Turned into a zombie,
Hope all will be fine,
Life perhaps, will take a turn,

For fortunes wrapped in time.

3) I often wonder

I often wonder
If all this is worth it,
If the light at the end
Of the tunnel

Is the source of joy,
Or the end of this
Fictitious bliss.

Days spent in solitude,
Thinking of this life,
Treading paths, seeking answers
In finding what is right.

I often wonder

"Will the pearly gates ever open?"

For this wandering soul,

Welcoming with open arms,

Waiting to embrace

Then flowers would bloom
In the gardens of my dreams,
With butterflies flitting all around

Making life complete.

I often wonder.

4) Laugh at me

Laugh at me
Make me cry
Live your life
Let me die.

Know your dreams
Make a wish
They'll come true
Then you'll fly.

Laugh at me
Feels so good
Some things can be
Understood

If you were me
And I were you
This game would end
Do not pretend

You may be god
I may be man
Laugh at me
I know your plan.

You set me up
Now I am damned
Break the spell
That you slammed

Laugh at me
What you do best
Let me go
I've passed the test

5) Stranger

I look into the mirror
And see a stranger's face,
It's not the person that I knew
Before starting the race.

I was always loving me
That time can't be replaced,
Life has brought me now and here
And caught me in this place.

Stranger I am mirror mirror,
Stranger to none but me,
Stranger to everything around,
Stranger to destiny.

Time's good now, not like it was
Should I now be happy?
Stranger I am to none but me,
Speaking in soliloquy.

In years I've changed, time and again
Then they turn back and see,
Make me look at what has gone
To greet eventually.

Stranger I am to none but me
Seeking my sanity,
Stranger I am to none but me
Waiting in line to be set free.

The stranger smiles at me
And says "Do you really know me?
Or is it that we just happen
To share a similarity."

"You look as if we've met before
Ages have gone you see,
You are not you anymore
And neither am I me."

I look the last time honestly
My eyes look into me,
Stranger I am to everything
And yet no one can see.

Dark Poems

1) Hello Satan

Hello Satan
How do you do?
You've taught me so much
That now I'm black 'n blue.

We've been real good friends,
Through thick and through thin.
You've shown me the world,
Now I'm left to spin.

Hello Satan
How do you do?
I've been through so much now,
That I know what is true.

The happiness that I run for
Is many miles ahead,
The moment that I reach it,
I find you there instead.

Hello Satan
How do you do?
I know what you're up to,
Your tricks are but a few.

Sometimes when there's sunshine,
You've made it my day.
I'm left with some options,
They'll help me in some way.

Hello Satan
How do you do?
The darkness allures me,
Welcomes me your way.

I can't seem to leave you,
You're feeling the same,
That's why I am here now
It's part of your game.

2) Slaves And Masters

Caught in a world
Of confusion,
Wanting to be free
All the time.

Humans trapping
Your emotions,
Fate trying to fail
Your life every time.

We are all instruments
Of the music
Played by others,
Week by week,

Either you're
The hunter,
Or the hunted
On the streets.

Slaves and masters,
Sophisticated evil ways,
Mind control in captivating souls
Cruel intentions the only goals.

There's no escaping,
The space is too vast,
The spell was cast
From zero to infinity.

No more light
Only gaping holes,
Slaves and masters
From eternity to eternity..

3) Chaos and confusion

Scattered thoughts,
Mindless deeds,
Uncertain fate
With a soul that pleads.

Careless wanderings,
Faithless meanderings,
Helpless God,
Endless needs.

Hope for meaning,
In place and time,
When Chaos and confusion
Possess the mind.

Reasons are lost,
When dreams are tossed,
With chaos and confusion,
Obsessed and blind.

Take me now,
Far away
Need some space
To find a day.

Let me row,
Let me grow,
Chaos and confusion,
Let me know.

Need to make it,
Mind of clay,
Chaos and confusion
Go away.

Teach me everything,
One last wish,
Before you decide to
Diffuse and vanish.

4) Black hole (Part 1)

Surely, there's a way out
Of this endless pit.
I'm thinking whether to shout,
Right here as I sit.

It was fine till the time
That this moment arrived,
The black hole took it all from me,
But still I survived.

This complexity of life
Has left me quite numb,
I have understood some things,
But still I am dumb.

Somehow, now I believe
In the power of God,
Otherwise I'm confounded,
By the arrogance of this flood.

The darkness devastates,
Yet the hope of escaping
Escalates... again and again.
While looking at the blackhole
With ever growing disdain.

As it regains
Its thirst for my blood,
I wait for some happiness that
Still doesn't give a nod.

I look for a way out,
But the black hole moves
Wherever I go,
And clings to me
Just like a shadow.

It's taken my joys,
My desires, and also
Bits and pieces of my mind.
I have to get out,

A way I must find.

So I act a little kind,
Self speculate, and remind
Myself of my good consideration,
And start a conversation

With the black hole.

5) Black hole (Part 2)

"Why are you doing this to me
Can I not be free?
I've been caught in this trap
What have I done?
Loosen this strap!!!"

The Black hole was silent.
For a while it seemed
That it had not heard
My cries or my screams.

Then a deep resonating sound
Emanated from the ground,
Sending with a quiver,
Shivers down my spine.

"You asked for it"
A deep voice said
"I was far away,
You called me here instead."

Was caught by surprise
At least the black hole spoke,
My hopes began to rise with happiness,
That my feelings recognized.

"How could I call you?
I never even knew you.
You just came by one day,
Since then, all you've done is stay."

The black hole rumbled
As it saw me so meek,
Although it had crumbled
By its own weight, it did speak.

"You asked for it"
The Black hole repeated
"It's all in your mind
What you choose, is what you shall find."

(.. To be continued)

Spiritual Poems

1) Meeting with the devil

I had a meeting with the Devil
Once again today,
He had a few things to tell me
If I may so say.

He reviewed all the motives
Required for the play,
And then he told me what to do
To make a busy day.

I had a meeting with the Devil
Once again today.

We talked on along the way
I had to stop and pray,
And think of all the reasons that
Had prompted him to stay.

What he told me
All seemed so true,
And things were crystal clear
He put his arms around me then
And often said "My Dear",

I had a meeting with the Devil
Once again today.

"Angels are of no use my friend,
They make your life so drab
Be with me and you will see
That life is really fab!"

"The fun is in just letting go
Who really is a Saint,
Many have ended their quest
'Boredom' was their complaint"

"Life is meant to just be free
That is, without a care,
Take the easy way to get,
All that you wanted 'Dear'

He was with me for quite some time
And then he said "I'll go,"
"I'll meet you once again when
You are weak down till your toe".

I have been thinking all this while
Of what happened since then,
I'll just do what is right for now
Till he appears again.

The angels have come out I guess
They have something to say,

They know I had a meeting with
The Devil once again.

Sunil Bhatia

2) Wandering Soul

After having lived my life
I park my ferry now,
Ravaged by many a storm
I make it out somehow.

There was a reason why I tried
To fight my destiny,
It was somewhat in my control
Before it now I bow.

I am a wandering soul,
Wandering soul, wandering soul
Only a spirit nine to nine,
Nine to nine, nine to nine.

I am a wandering soul
Wandering through this flight,
Only a spirit nine to nine,
Waiting to alight.

I touched many forbidden shores
Not wished for by my kind,
The thirst of my lonely being
Had left them far behind.

I reached the nadir of my life
Not by one, but with many a tide,
Every time challenged when I rose,
My knowledge multiplied.

I am a wandering soul
Knowing I am blind,
Surrounded by the infinite,
Perhaps with second sight.

I have the magic of
Divinity all around,
Living in the physical world
Between the heavens and the ground

Fortunes reversed,
The truth dawned
Questions many
Were answered.

There was a light, it looked so bright
It came to comfort me,
It was unknown, something happened
Was all that I could see.

I am a wandering soul
Wandering soul, wandering soul,
I am a wandering soul
Wandering through the sky.

Everything that comes will pass
Yet I will never die.

3) Mind trip (The Journey)

Let me take you now,
On a journey of the mind,
A place that you may like
Somewhere that you might find.

Happiness, love, and
All you've always wanted,
Care, and all above
The things you've always planted.

So, close your eyes
And think that you're there,
It's a journey of the senses
A mind trip of surprise.

Float, your thoughts,
Yes, there's no care
The mind trip is so wonderful,
It's living here and there.

Don't deny,
The good things you've desired,
So reach in to your heart and soul,
And spread out inner fires.

Live in new dimensions,
Experience joy and fun,
The mind trip is so beautiful,
Life will soon gone.

But

The journey will go on.

4) Trance

Open your eyes,
Tell me what you see
Dreams that you dreamt of,
Your reality.

Leave your connection
With misery,
Turn your direction to
Your destiny.

Open your eyes
Know what you need,
Happiness in everything
Lies in leaving greed.

Do not remember
All that you regret,
Time to surrender
All that you suspect.

Open your eyes
Time to be wise
Breathe what you live for
Self hypnotize.

Trance in a moment
Cycles of joy
Fountains of happiness
Where angels fly.

Darkness surrounds us
Stars in the sky
Trance is religion
Consciousness high.

Sunil Bhatia

God is rewarding
For those who try
Once you have known him
Don't pass him by.

Free inhibitions
Once more arrive
Hell will forgive you
If you survive.

Open your eyes
Tell what you see
Let the trance take you
Where you want to be.

5) The Fallen Angel

Programmed by fate and destiny,
Living with the hope of choice
For continuity,

The fallen angel,
Goes into oblivion.
With no directions, no sensations.

Love is a probability,
Living in some anomaly
Created by distorted equations
In the symphony of life.

The fallen angel rises,
From its ashes of the past
With nowhere to go,

Except with thoughts,
Flying in search of happiness,
But somewhere it knows,

This coincidence of errors,
Is yet another chance,
The fallen angel moves on,

Resurrecting itself from the clutches
Of incoherent dreams.
To embrace the freedom

Of the infinite realm.

Inspirational Poems

1) Spaces (Abstract Poetry)

Things done years ago
Are saving me today
Feelings comfort me
And help me pave the way.

Many things, many reasons
Restlessly lead again
Seldom won, mostly gone
Victory survives

Amidst peace from forgotten joys.

Then

Spaces, empty spaces
Come into my life,
Thoughts lost in the past
Return and bring some sunshine.

Plastic life, plastic smiles
Made by demons
Waiting to devour
My freedom of choice.

Emotions mixed with
All sorts of experiences
Create madness not
Easy to explain.

Destiny wanting to defeat me
Returns again to play.
Tired by situations
Knowing not what to do.

I find these spaces
Empty spaces
That bring me
Back again.

Spaces, empty spaces
Make me alive.
Again.

2) Happiness

Happiness in sunshine,

Happiness in rain,

Happiness in happiness,

Happiness in pain.

Can be found between

Such is time again.

Happiness is seen

But it can't be feigned.

Happiness in four walls

Opens window panes,

Happiness is madness

Let loose, thoughts contained,

Happiness for someone

Puts loneliness to shame

Happiness in everything,

Is happiness's game.

Happiness a stranger,

For those left in chains

Happiness the reason

Is all left to gain.

Happiness will make you

The child there within,

Happiness will take you

Away from all sin.

Happiness will grow you
A garden within

Where wild bees and flowers

And butterflies can swim.

Happiness will reap your

Harvest like a scythe,

Sometime feel that happiness

Is nothing more

Than a myth.

3) The Ship

There was a Ship
Upon a sea
It had a crew
Of seventy.

It had been out
For many months
It had not seen
The coast at for long.

The captain said
"The sails are spread
There is no wind
Use oars instead."

"We have to live
We have to move
Or we'll run short
Of all our bread."

There was a Ship
Upon a sea
It had a crew
Of seventy.

The compass showed
North north west
The sun had reached
Its time of rest

Throughout the day
There was no soul
No birds around
Just empty holes

And miles and miles
Of splashing waves
Which crashed upon
The wooden cage.

A sailor took
The telescope
And ran his eyes
Around the rails

No sign of any
Moving sound
No ship no trees
Not even clouds

And everything
Appeared so dead
The sky itself
Was like a shroud.

There was a Ship
Upon a sea
It had a crew
Of seventy.

The crew were men
With wives at home
And they had longed
The shores to come

"Perhaps we'll die
If we don't reach.
This kind of life
Is killing me"

"Do not lose hope"
The Captain said
"We'll find our way
Just keep your head"

Sunil Bhatia

"You have been brave
A little more
Is what I ask
For you to be"

There was a Ship
Upon a sea
It had a crew
Of seventy.

The Ship was old
It seemed to creak
And many storms
Had made it weak

There was no hope
For days had passed
The ship began
To lose its mast.

It was the 100th
Day at sea
And all the crew
Still seventy.

Next day they saw
A bird alight
Its wooden post
It was a sight

Everybody
Jumped with joy
Together they shouted
"Land ahoy!!"

They found their life
Their families
And landed safe
After the strife.

The Ship was sent
To the Town Hall
A memory
For the folksmen all

Today it's just
A thought again
The Ship has gone
The tale remains.

4) Time Machine

Am feeling better now
Am feeling fine somehow

My thoughts were causing pain
They were caught in my brain

My heart cried out in vain
Time transcended again

Something had happened
It was in the past

The future's waiting
It isn't meant to last

Am feeling better now
Am feeling fine somehow

The clock is ticking
The time machine moves you
Like a fish

It moves you whenever you want
It moves you
wherever you wish

The flow of motion
Creates harmony

Feel the emotion
To suit your fancy

Somewhere in your senses
Life will leave it's trace

Release in the present
Float freely then in space

The time machine
Plays and rewinds

Be where you want to be
In destinies' chase

The time machine is working
Life is being kind

Be where you want to be
It's all in the mind.

Observational Poems

1) *Lies*

The world is a farce
And everything is lies
Most of what you see
Is by a human who dies.

Nature loves us
But we are to blame
We've won our battles
For chances to claim.

Lies an addiction
Lies are the fuel
Lies an attraction
Fit for a fool.

Lies liberate us
Like a clown, it's so cruel
Lies make a moment
Like a crown with its jewel.

Lies are the truth
And all truth denies
What we love the most
Stands up and replies.

Lies give us freedom
Lies are like god
Waiting in prison
To wield their rod.

Lies will embrace you
For you are their child
Lies will grace you
And save you from the wild.

Lies will take you
Up to your final ride
Because your life is just
A lie deep inside.

2) God, Man and Religion

God made
Man

Man made
Religion.

Religion united
Man

Many religions divided
Mankind.

Religion was
Devised

Is pristine advanced
Robotics

Which made
Clones

Overtaking our
Minds.

What a
Brilliant

Software
Programme

Which got
Corrupted

Somewhere along the
Timeline.

God made
Man

Man made
Religion.

God still
Laughs

Man still
Cries.

3) Rules of the game

Don't tell me,
Don't tell me,
The rules of the game,

You know it,
You know it,
They won't be the same.

I found out,
I found out,
You wanted to tame,

So be it,
So be it,
You can have your name.

Let's play it,
Let's play it,
Someone gets the fame,

Don't want them
Don't want them
Excuses are lame.

You can win,
You can win,
Although it's a shame,

Lets follow,
Lets follow,
The rules of the game.

4) Once upon a time

Once upon a time,
The smell of rain,
And the sound of rustling trees
In the wind
Mesmerized my mind.

There were moonlit rides,
In the fantasy of an unparalleled kind.

Once upon a time,
There was every thing,
That is treasured by a juvenile,

In the youth of happiness,
From the clutches of the world quarantined.

Once upon a time,
There was life running through
My veins, breath flowing through
My eyes,
Now only my soul survives.

Seeking salvation amidst
Silent cries that secretly drown,
The goodness and sounds,
That once shone, through our lives.

Once upon a time.

5) *I think I know what's happening*

I think I know what's happening,
Although much can't be said,
I think I know what's happening,
Some people can be read.

They may believe that they are smart,
Perhaps they really are,
I think I know what's happening,
I've understood the art.

The eyes they say a lot at times,
Even when lips have lied,

I think I know what's happening,
You can say that I spied.

A smile can say a lot although
It wasn't really meant,
I think I know what's happening,
And how your time was spent.

Although some words can change a mind
Left groping for some light,
I think I know what's happening,
Perhaps its second sight.

So be happy I will not show,
Your game that is well known,
I think I know what's happening,
Although nothing is shown.

Humorous Poems

1) I am a rat

I am a rat
Nibbling on the cheese in a trap
Laid down to catch me
By some ridiculous chap.

My nose sniffs around
As I hear the sound
Of stealthy steps
Tip toeing on the ground.

I am a rat
Chased by your lovely cat
She doesn't look too fat
Drat drat drat !!!

I am a rat
Scurrying across the mat,
Petrified by feet
Walking across the pavement
And the street.

And I'm the pest
So you act to eliminate
My little life, I'm not your guest
Such is the fact.

I am a rat
Searching for many a hole
All to save my soul
From humans,

To keep me intact.

Sunil Bhatia

You may say what you can
You're the best to live
Yet
I'm not your fan.

I am a rat,
Tell you what
Lousy man,
Catch me if you can.

2) Copenhagen (The UN Climate Change Conference, 2011)

Welcome brethren of equal lives
Also the lesser mortal souls
The richer nations have it all
The poorer ones can join or fall.

It's not easy to be on top
And sometimes we must learn to stop
The time has come as we proclaim
That life will never be the same.

This is our council, and our den
As we meet in Copenhagen.

We've bombed our planet left and right
And shown each other of our might
We've burnt fuel 24 by 7

We meet now in Copenhagen.

We've dumped our waste and cut our trees
And now have only rising seas
Since we have nuclear weapons now

We can meet in Copenhagen.

There's so much that we need to do
For we suffer, and others too
It is a fact and it is true
That skies have now a different hue.

Children won't see the oceans blue
And most of all that time is when
We may not be in power then
The time is ripe.. it's heaven sent

Sunil Bhatia

What matters dear is the G 10
If we only get your consent

We'll sail through in Copenhagen.

We'll grab our future, that's for sure
As fighting nations we want more
So what if there's war and famine?
Flooded streets and melting ice

Our lives are like a game of dice
And winners have to pay a price.

So let us make the best of time
Have gourmet food, cheese and wine

We are the makers of our fate
And hold the keys to our own gate
We may not live to meet again

For now we have Copenhagen

3) Davos (The World Economic Forum 2012)

We did it, we did it,
We did it, this time
Burnt holes in our pockets
Hearing the bells chime.

Pardon me Sir/Ma'am,
Don't mean to offend,
No nickels and dimes
Are left now to spend.

With tottering economies
That once spoke of trust
Their bubbles are bursting
In oceans of dust.

There are no free lunches
For heaven's sake please
We've gorged on our money
Now life is a tease.

For words we're at a loss
Things gone for a toss
It was your fault boss
Don't lie in Davos.

It started with Greece
Now Europe is bad
Such perplexity
Is driving us mad.

Everything was great
Till 2008
No one's left to bait
Such is now the state.

Sunil Bhatia

There was the sweet sound
Of dollars and pounds
Can't hear much around
As we hit the ground.

Let us vow to cure
Us of this disease
Jobs can be created
With lives on a lease.

Be rain hail or snow
On must be the show
Its time to be honest
Credit gave the blow.

I'd like some more champagne
It makes me feel high
Lord I know we're sinking
It makes me feel dry.

Now that we have toasted
To all we had boasted
Let us fingers cross
Here now in Davos.

2012 has arrived
Not much left to pride
There must be an answer
Search deep down inside.

We've been running now
From pillar to post
To save our currencies
What we love the most.

One day then will come
Again we'll have fun
Let's play till that time
Get on with the crime.

4) Corporate Jargon

Was going through the
SOP's and compliance reports
That were critical for our
Companies' profitability.

The GOP had shrunk so much so
That cost cutting was inevitable
Redeployment of the workforce had
Become the order of the day.

Several manuals had been consulted
And training's had been organized
To infuse fresh energy in the workplace
For unleashing the manpower potential to its fullest.

Our strategy to outdo our competition
Was in line with
The vision & mission statement
Of our Organization.

The beliefs, motto and goals were
Also to be re looked at as the
Management mantras and resource
Allocations were not productive any longer.

It was observed that
The life span graph of our
Brand indicated a fatigue factor
That had crept in the minds of
Our key clientele.

Market analysis further
Revealed that the perceived
Value proposition of our presentations
Did not appeal to our target audience

Sunil Bhatia

Which resulted in their
Migrating to better showcased
Products and services thereby
Affecting our fiscal budget.

The conclusion is that we
Need to be capital and labor
Intensive and have to build
Loyalty over our networking and
Information distribution channels.

Our existing offerings have
To be innovated
And improvised to get
The desired results.

Once we enhance our data base
With new alliances and acquisitions
It would enable us in aligning
Our core competencies thus

Allowing us to achieve our targets.

Once our funds flow statements
Are in sync with our asset allocations
This would eventually help fueling
Our year on year growth projections

We would then get a 360° analysis
Of our progress

And show healthier charts
That are mandatory for us
To get the requisite media
Attention for our future prospects.

Amen.

5) Consumer Babble

Let me buy your
Fairness cream
Your fancy cars
Your Bank loan dreams.

I have a craving
In my heart
To have it all
Right now it seems.

The Fashion stores
Elitist doors
The Foodie joints
The 'Have it all' points.

Let me buy your
'Must have' thoughts
For just a moment
Of all sorts.

The Shopping malls
Couture draped halls
The happy voices
In the stalls.

I have desires
Deep down now
To spend my savings
One and all.

For all that you
Have there for me
Whether I need it
Actually.

Sunil Bhatia

The Socialist streak
Spend thrift at ease
"A tenderloin steak
For me please!"

This is the epitome
Of our lives
In pools of wants
We take our dives.

I'm not easy
To satisfy
Don't need no more
Now that's lie.

I am a specimen
Of your choice
You got me now
You can rejoice.

I've had enough
Now I'll refrain.
Let me go now
Call me again.

Futuristic Poems

1) Robot

I am a Robot
Living logically
My life is smooth
Such is my machinery.

I've been programmed
By a higher energy
I will perform
It's built in my circuitry.

I have no emotions
Its meant that way
For I am a part
Of the money making factory.

My controls are with
My Company
I live for them
But nobody lives for me.

I am a Robot
Is this my destiny?

I must wake up
Its part of my integrity
Sleep is a stranger
To be human is a falsity.

Keep moving
Till you make it to the top
The profits may come down a' falling
So there's no way that you can ever stop.

Sunil Bhatia

There is no love
When you're chasing dimes
The only rest is
When they unplug our minds.

I am a Robot
I'll outdate with time
Some new technology
Will leave me far behind.

I only hope
That I survive this climb
For I am just a Robot
And I come with a life line.

I need to be serviced now
It's part of the design
And the only truth is
That one day I will just be.

Nothing more than
A rusty tin can
Lying in a backyard
Waiting for the van.

2) Man from the future

Who knows what will happen
When the clock ticks tic tock tic,
The days are dead and dreary
The nights are playing tricks.

It's all so obvious that the truth
Will stand up nice and tall,
The man from the future
Has somehow seen it all.

Perhaps he's there amidst the crowd,
Looking at the past,
Knowing where the world will go
Till the time it lasts.

The man from the future
Will return to his land,
Only to come back one day
To see if all's as planned.

3) Clones Vs Robots.

Many years from now,
After being born several times
In laboratories sponsored,
Biology in technological crime,

There would be only two clans.
Clones Vs Robots.
Both creations of the human mind.

Who would win?
To see that prime,
When federations would trade
Inconsiderate of all mankind.

Clones Vs Robots,
Fighting for supremacy
In finding the cure
To end mediocrity.

Clones Vs Robots,
Who will survive?
The future has the answer
If allowed to arrive.

4) Time Machine

Am feeling better now
Am feeling fine somehow

My thoughts were causing pain
They were caught in my brain

My heart cried out in vain
Time transcended again

Something had happened
It was in the past

The future's waiting
It isn't meant to last

Am feeling better now
Am feeling fine somehow

The clock is ticking
The time machine moves you
Like a fish

It moves you whenever you want
It moves you
Wherever you wish

The flow of motion
Creates harmony

Feel the emotion
To suit your fancy

Somewhere in your senses
Life will leave it's trace

Sunil Bhatia

Release in the present
Float freely then in space

The time machine
Plays and rewinds

Be where you want to be
In destinies' chase

The time machine is working
Life is being kind

Be where you want to be
It's all in the mind.

5) Cyber Wars

Make a post, make one more
Don't lose ground, hope for more
Click the button, to the room
Open the window, you are doomed.

Cyber wars, paralyzing brains
Humans caught for others' gains
Cyber wars, killer space
Annihilating all the human race.

Many players at this time
Waiting at the scene of crime
Wanting to deceive you now,
With their wily wicked minds.

Cyber wars have got you now
You've been made, their cash cow,
Pushing patterns, look confused?
Mind seizure, turn to be used.

Couch potato, techno geek
Loss of sunshine, looking meek
Cross fired without a dime
Wasted now, for a lifetime

Cyber wars are in command
You are part of the demand
Pulling virtually, has resumed
Run before you are consumed.

Eat popcorn, watch TV
Go for movies, mobile sleek,
Electronic life, looking green
Get yourself stuck in your screen

Sunil Bhatia

Cyber wars fought day and night,
Add new convicts what a plight
You can't run, nor can you hide
You can browse, but you can't decide.

Save your life, see what's real
Life was yours, they've got a steal,
Raking profits, addicts slow
Prisoners of the modern show.

Cyber wars, part of the game
You are just a pawn in the frame
They will win, you will lose
There's still time, for you to choose.

End of Part 1